Simple Tarts

Simple Tarts

Sweet and savory recipes
for all occasions

Elizabeth Wolf-Cohen

CHARTWELL
BOOKS, INC.

A QUINTET BOOK

Published by Chartwell Books, Inc.
A Division of Book Sales, Inc.
114 Northfield Avenue
Edison, New Jersey 08837

This edition produced for sale in the U.S.A., its
territories and dependencies only.

ISBN 0-7858-0746-2

This book was designed and produced by
Quintet Publishing Limited
6 Blundell Street
London N7 9BH

Creative Director: Richard Dewing
Designer: Isobel Gillan
Project Editor: Anna Briffa
Editor: Barbara Croxford
Photographer: Tim Hill

Typeset in Great Britain by
Central Southern Typesetters, Eastbourne
Manufactured in Malaysia by C.H. Colourscan Sdn Bhd
Printed in China by Leefung-Asco Printers Ltd

CONTENTS

INTRODUCTION

Simple Tarts is a book for pastry lovers and those who love simple fresh food. Tarts have an appealing freshness which underlines a tasty filling that can be sweet or savory.

Tarts, or open pastry shells, play a part in many culinary traditions, but have played a very important part in American, British, and French cuisines. Often called open- or single-crust pies in the USA, tarts can easily form the basis of simple desserts such as a fresh berry tart, or an elaborate sweet such as the Mocha Mousse Slice. Leek and Onion Tartlets or Mussel and Leek Tart make a substantial main course. In fact, tarts make an ideal showcase for an amazing variety of foods.

Most of these tarts are easy to prepare and, with a little forethought, can be put together quickly. Remember pastry can be bought from supermarkets and homemade pastry freezes well, so make it in batches and freeze ahead. Fillings can be assembled in no time, so use your imagination and enjoy the treat of a simple tart made with delicious tender pastry, warm from the oven.

Every cook I know aspires to make light, tender flaky pastry. There are a few basic commandments that must always be obeyed, regardless of what kind of pastry you choose:

● Chill all the ingredients (my pastry teacher used to keep a bag of flour in the freezer!).

● Work as quickly as possible and, unless you are one of those natural born pastry makers, use a pastry blender (instead of two knives) or use the ideal tool – a food processor.

● Chill the dough after every stage of making and assembling: Chill after patting into a disc and after rolling out and lining the tart or pie pan. Do not be tempted to cheat – your pastry will shrink unevenly.

● Pastry likes a hot oven; butter-rich pastries and puff pastry especially require a hot blast of heat to seal the pastry and release the steam. If longer cooking is required for a filling, the temperature can be reduced so the pastry does not burn.

THE INGREDIENTS

Most kinds of pastry are made with a combination of flour, fat, and a liquid to bind. The texture, flavor, and color of the resulting pastry will vary tremendously depending on the proportions and types of ingredients used.

Flour

All-purpose flour is available nationwide and is used throughout this book. Even the same brand of flour can vary from season to season, depending on humidity or how long it has been stored, however, so the amount of liquid necessary to bind the dough will always vary. I use the "scoop and sweep" method of measuring. Dip a solid cup measure into a container of flour and, using a broad-bladed knife, level off the excess flour; ⅛ teaspoon baking powder can be added to 1 cup flour to achieve a lighter result. Whole-wheat or rye flour can replace some of the white flour in savory pastry, but produces a heavier result. Use equal amounts or more white flour proportionally to whole-wheat or other flours for easier handling.

Fat

Lard was probably the first fat used in pastry making, but has fallen out of favor for health reasons. It does make a very short and tender pastry, but has a distinctive taste. White vegetable fat or "Crisco" has virtually replaced lard, although it is generally combined with butter or margarine. My personal choice is butter. Pure butter gives pastry a richer flavor and color and a crisper texture, but it can be difficult to handle. Most cooks use a combination of butter or hard margarine (not the soft tub variety) and white vegetable fat to achieve a balance of good buttery color and flavor with the short flaky texture provided by white fat. I use "sweet", or unsalted, butter because it has a lower water content and the amount of salt can be more easily controlled. Experiment until you find your own preference.

The normal proportion of fat to flour is usually half fat to flour (i.e. one part fat to two parts flour), although some rich European-style pastries such as Pâte Sucrée have a higher percentage of fat. The more fat the dough has, the more difficult it will be to handle, so be sure the dough is chilled at all stages of handling.

Liquid

Most pastry is bound with water, although milk or other liquids can be used. Normal tart pastry uses about 1 teaspoon of water per ounce of flour; this varies if eggs or an egg yolk is added. The water should be iced water so it does not melt or soften the fats. Too much water will make a sticky dough, which is difficult to handle and makes tough pastry. Be careful when using a food processor, since the mixture can form into a dough before the correct quantity of liquid has been added. This can produce a dough that is too short and is difficult to handle and produces a brittle, too crumbly, pastry. Many recipes call for an egg yolk mixed with water to a certain measure. This adds a golden color and helps to bind the pastry. Sometimes a little juice is added for flavor, but be careful as certain juices such as lemon contain a high proportion of acid, which can shorten the pastry too much for easy handling. A little grated orange or lemon zest should add just the right kind of flavor. Extracts such as vanilla, almond, or lemon can be used to enhance the chosen fillings, as can spices such as cinnamon, nutmeg, ginger, or cardamom.

Eggs

Eggs are added to pastry doughs for richness in texture and flavor, and because they help bind the pastry. Normally only the yolk is used and some rich doughs use only yolks to produce a very rich cookie-like pastry used in some European-style tarts.

Sugar

Sugar is used both to sweeten the final pastry and create a crisper texture. A teaspoon or two is often added even to savory doughs, because the sugar helps the pastry to color and gives a more golden look. Superfine sugar or confectioners' sugar is generally used because these types dissolve more quickly. Granulated sugar can be used but can result in a crunchy texture not always desired.

Store-Bought Pastry

Excellent quality pie crust, puff pastry, and phyllo pastry can be purchased in supermarkets and all give good reliable results. Puff pastry is available chilled or frozen and gives excellent results. Look for the all-butter variety since the flavor is superior. Phyllo pastry is also available chilled or frozen and is a great freezer stand-by. These paper-thin sheets of dough need to be defrosted before being carefully unwrapped. Because the thin layers dry so quickly, they should be covered with a damp dishtowel when working.

chapter one

MAKING PASTRY

Although many good-quality, store-bought pastries are available, there is nothing quite as satisfying as making your own. The method for making a Basic Pie Crust is easy to follow and, once mastered, can be adapted for both sweet and savory tarts simply by adding a few extra ingredients.

BASIC PIE CRUST (Pâte Brisée)

Brisée in French means broken. In this pie crust the flour and fats are "broken together," or cut in. After adding the liquid, the dough is blended until the mixture begins to bind together. If the dough becomes sticky at any stage, refrigerate until it is easy to handle. This recipe should produce a firm yet flaky crust which can support a filling yet is tender. Sifting flour is not absolutely necessary, but can help lighten the pastry if you use the hand method.

Ingredients

• For a 9- or 10-inch tart pan

• 1¼ cups all-purpose flour
• ½ tsp salt
• 1 tsp superfine sugar, optional
• 6 tbsp cold unsalted butter, cut into small pieces
• 2 tbsp cold margarine or white vegetable fat, cut into small pieces
• 2–4 tbsp iced water

Hand Method

1 Into a large bowl, sift the flour, salt, and sugar if using. Sprinkle the pieces of butter and margarine or white vegetable fat over the flour mixture. Using a pastry blender or two knives scissor-fashion, cut in the fat until the mixture forms coarse crumbs. Do not overwork, as this causes a tough crust.

2 Sprinkle about 2 tablespoons of the water over the flour-crumb mixture and toss lightly with a fork. Gather the parts of dough that have bound together to one side of the bowl. Add a little more water to any dry crumbs and toss again.

3 Gather the dough into a rough ball and turn onto a sheet of plastic wrap. Using the plastic wrap as a guide, lightly press the dough into a disc shape and flatten slightly. Wrap dough tightly and refrigerate about 1 hour or overnight.

Food Processor Method

If you have warm hands, are working in hot weather, tend to have a heavy touch, or just have not got the knack, the food processor should be the answer to your prayers. Used carefully, it produces perfect dough every time; just take care not to overprocess. Although Pâte Brisée is easily made by hand, the sweeter doughs do benefit from the food processor method. The more sugar and fat added to the dough, the more difficult it is to handle.

1 Put the flour, salt, and sugar in the bowl of a food processor fitted with the metal blade. Process 5–7 seconds just to blend. Sprinkle the pieces of butter and margarine or white vegetable fat over the surface and process 10–15 seconds until the mixture resembles coarse crumbs.

2 Sprinkle 2 tablespoons of the water over the flour-crumb mixture and, using the pulse button, process the mixture until the dough just begins to hold together, 10–15 seconds. DO NOT OVERPROCESS. Test the dough by pinching a piece between your fingers. If it is still too crumbly, add more water, little by little, and pulse again until the dough begins to stick together in clumps. Do not allow the dough to form into a ball or add too much water because the pastry will be tough. Turn the dough onto a sheet of plastic wrap and continue with step 3 on page 9.

ROLLING AND SHAPING THE DOUGH

If the dough has been refrigerated for more than an hour, allow it to soften slightly at room temperature for about 10 minutes.

To Form a Dough Circle

1 Unwrap the dough and place on a lightly floured surface. Using a lightly floured rolling pin, press a row of parallel grooves into the dough. Turn the dough 45°, flouring the surface underneath and press another row of parallel grooves. Continue

rotating and pressing the dough, being careful the dough does not stick, until the dough is about ½ inch thick. This method avoids overworking the dough before actually rolling it.

2 Beginning from the center, lightly roll out the dough to the far edge, but do not actually roll over the edge. Return to the center and roll to the near edge, but do not roll over the edge. Turn the dough 45° and continue rolling until dough is about ⅛ inch thick and forms a 12-inch round. Do not allow the dough to stick to the surface; lightly flour the surface and rolling pin as necessary using a small pastry brush to remove any excess flour from the dough.

> **TIP:** *To freeze rolled-out pastry dough, carefully slide onto a flat baking sheet and freeze, uncovered, until very firm. Remove from freezer and slide onto freezer paper, wrap well and refreeze, with paper in between each layer. Wrap tightly and store in the freezer. Defrost in the refrigerator overnight or at room temperature several hours before using.*

3 If the dough is tender or tears, patch it with a small piece of moistened dough. As the dough circle enlarges, fold it in half or into quarters to rotate and dust with flour to avoid stretching the dough.

To Form a Square or Rectangle

Proceed as above but rotate the dough 90° rather than 45° when making the grooves. This will cause the dough to elongate to fill a square or rectangular pan.

Lining a Tart Pan

The traditional tart pan is shallow with no rim. It usually has a fluted side and removeable bottom that gives the characteristic edge and allows the side of the pan to be removed for presentation without disturbing the base. Flan rings are generally smooth-sided rings which are set on a heavy pastry sheet to form its bottom; these are generally used by professionals. The best pans are dull metal or non-stick since shiny metal reflects the heat and prevents the crust from browning properly. Butter-rich dough does not generally stick, but I like to lightly spray the tart pan with a vegetable cooking spray. Alternatively, brush the bottom and side of the tart pan with a little oil.

1 To transfer rolled-out dough to a tart pan, set the rolling pin on the near edge of the pastry round, square, or rectangle. Fold the edge of the pastry over the rolling pin, then continue to roll dough loosely around pin.

2 Hold far edge of dough and rolling pin over far edge of the tart pan and gently unroll the dough, allowing it to settle into the pan without stretching or pulling.

3 Using floured fingertips, lift outside edge of dough and ease into bottom and side of pan, allowing excess pastry to overhang the edge. Smooth the pastry onto the bottom of the pan and press the overhang down slightly towards the center of the pan, making the top edge thicker.

4 Roll the rolling pin over the edge, cutting off any excess dough and flattening the top edge. Press the thickened top edge against the side of the pan to form a stand-up edge. This makes the edge slightly thicker and higher, reinforcing the side of the pastry shell. Prick the bottom of the dough with a fork and, if you like, crimp or decorate the edge. Refrigerate 1 hour or freeze for 20 minutes.

Lining Tartlet Pans

For very small tartlet pans (less than 2 inches), arrange the pans on the work surface close together and unroll the rolled-out pastry over them, loosely draping the dough into them. Roll the rolling pin over them to cut off the excess pastry then, using a floured thumb, press the pastry onto the bottom and up the side of the pans. Prick bottoms with a fork.

For larger tartlets, I prefer to follow the steps for lining a round tart pan, since this gives adequate pastry and a firm high edge to support any filling.

Blind Baking

Blind baking is a method of pre-baking a pastry case, either partially or completely, to prevent the pastry from becoming soggy and to ensure that the base cooks evenly.

1 Cut out a circle of wax paper or foil about 3 inches larger than the tart pan. Fold the paper or foil in half and lay it across the center of the dough-lined tart pan. Unfold it and press onto the bottom, into the edge, and up the side of the dough.

2 Fill the paper- or foil-lined tart shell with dried beans, rice, or pastry weights, being careful to spread them evenly over the bottom and up the side. The dried beans, rice, or pastry weights can be cooled and saved to be used again.

3 To partially blind bake pastry: bake in a 400°F oven for 15–20 minutes until the pastry is set and the rim looks dry and slightly golden. Carefully remove to a heatproof surface and remove the paper or foil and beans. The pastry shell can now be filled and baking finished.

4 To completely blind bake pastry: bake in a 400°F oven for 10 minutes. Remove to an ovenproof surface and carefully remove the paper or foil and beans. Gently prick the pastry bottom again with a fork and continue baking for 5–10 minutes until golden. The bottom should look dry and set. Cool completely on a wire rack before filling.

RICH PIE CRUST (Pâte Brisée Riche)

Ingredients
- For a 10-inch tart pan

- 1¼ cups all-purpose flour
- ½ tsp salt
- ½ cup (1 stick) cold unsalted butter, cut into small pieces
- 1 egg yolk beaten with 2 tbsp iced water

Proceed as for Basic Pie Crust (Pâte Brisée) using the beaten egg yolk and water to bind.

RICH HERB PIE CRUST

This tender green-flecked pastry is ideal for savory tarts. Vary the herbs to suit the filling and your taste.

Ingredients
- For a 10-inch tart pan

- 1¼ cups all-purpose flour
- ½ tsp salt
- ½ cup (1 stick) cold unsalted butter
- ½ tsp fresh thyme leaves or
- ¼ tsp dried thyme
- ½ tsp fresh oregano or marjoram chopped or
- ¼ tsp dried oregano or marjoram
- 2 tbsp chopped chives
- 1 tbsp fresh parsley, chopped
- 4–6 fresh basil leaves, torn into small pieces
- 1 egg yolk beaten with 2 tbsp iced water

Prepare as for Rich Pie Crust, adding the herbs when the flour and butter have been combined to form coarse crumbs, and before adding the water.

LIGHT WHOLE-WHEAT PIE CRUST

This whole-wheat crust remains light and flaky by substituting less than half the white flour for whole-wheat. Substitute 1 tablespoon of white vegetable fat for the butter if you would like to produce a very flaky pastry.

Ingredients

- For a 10-inch tart pan

- ¾ cup all-purpose flour
- ½ cup whole-wheat flour
- ½ tsp salt
- 3 tbsp cold unsalted butter, cut into small pieces
- 1 tbsp white vegetable fat or hard margarine
- 1 egg yolk beaten with 2 tbsp iced water

Proceed as for Basic Pie Crust combining the two flours and salt before cutting in the fats.

BASIC SWEET CRUST (Pâte Sucrée)

Pâte Sucrée, "sweetened pastry", is made in the same way as Pâte Brisée but contains more sugar and is generally bound with egg yolks or a combination of egg yolks and water. I use confectioners' sugar because it dissolves instantly, but superfine sugar can also be used. These additions make the pastry sweeter and a little crisper, which is ideal for dessert and fruit tarts. After the dough is formed, it is lightly kneaded by a process called "fresage" where the heel of the hand blends the dough until it is soft and pliable. The addition of sugar and egg yolk makes the pastry softer and more difficult to handle, so be sure to chill all the ingredients and work quickly. However, because this is a soft dough, it is easy to patch; just press any tears together – they will not show. This pastry can be made by hand by following the instructions for Pâte Brisée but I prefer to use the food processor and find the results equally satisfying.

Ingredients

- For a 9- or 10-inch tart pan or ten 3-inch tartlet pans

- 1 cup all-purpose flour
- ½ tsp salt
- 3–4 tbsp confectioners' sugar
- ½ cup (1 stick) cold unsalted butter, cut into small pieces
- 2 egg yolks beaten with 2 tbsp iced water and ½ tsp vanilla extract (optional)

1 Put the flour, salt and sugar in the bowl of a food processor, fitted with the metal blade. Process 5–7 seconds. Sprinkle the butter over the flour mixture and process 10–15 seconds until the mixture resembles coarse crumbs. Pulse 2–3 times more if the crumbs are not evenly distributed.

2 With the machine running, pour the yolk-water mixture through the feed tube and process just until dough begins to hold together. DO NOT OVERPROCESS.

Test the dough by pinching a piece between your fingers. If it is still crumbly add a little more water and pulse once or twice. Do not allow the dough to form into a ball at this stage because the pastry will become tough. Turn the dough out onto a sheet of plastic wrap.

3 Using the plastic wrap as a guide, hold each side with one hand and gently push the dough away from you, turning the dough and holding the opposite sides of the plastic wrap to contain it, until the dough is smooth and just blended. Flatten the dough into a circle and wrap with the plastic wrap. Refrigerate for 1 hour or overnight.

For a Light Nut Crust add 2–3 tablespoons finely chopped nuts to the flour mixture before adding any liquid.

EXTRA SWEET TART CRUST
(Pâte Sucrée Riche)

With a little more sugar and egg yolk, pastry becomes a melting, rich cookie or shortbread dough, that is ideal for fruit tarts and tartlets. This dough is very tricky to handle; although chilling is important, do not chill for too long or it will be too hard to roll out. If you cannot roll it out, simply press it in the tart pan using your flour-dipped fingers.

Ingredients

- For a 9-inch tart pan

- 1 cup all-purpose flour
- ½ tsp salt
- 4–5 tbsp confectioners' sugar
- ½ cup (1 stick) cold unsalted butter, cut into small pieces
- 3 egg yolks, beaten with 1 tbsp iced water and ½ tsp vanilla extract (optional)

Proceed as for Pâte Sucrée.

EASY NUT CRUST

This is a delicious flavorful crust, which makes an ideal base for custards and cooked fillings. It does not need rolling out and can be pressed straight into a tart pan with lightly floured hands, chilled, and then baked without weighting.

Ingredients

- For a 9-inch tart pan

- 1 cup (2 sticks) unsalted butter at room temperature
- 1 egg, lightly beaten
- 1 tsp vanilla or almond extract (optional)
- 1½ cups all-purpose flour
- ½ tsp sugar
- 1 cup finely chopped walnuts, pecans, almonds, hazelnuts, or macadamia nuts

1 Lightly spray or brush the tart pan with a vegetable cooking spray or a little melted butter or oil.

2 Using an electric mixer, cream the butter in a large bowl. Add the egg and vanilla extract and beat until blended. Sprinkle over the flour, sugar, and nuts and beat on low speed until well-blended.

3 Scrape the dough into the prepared pan and press evenly onto the bottom and up the side of the tart pan or pie plate. Using a fork, prick the bottom of the dough. Place in a refrigerator and chill for at least 30 minutes.

4 Preheat the oven to 350°F. Bake about 20 minutes or until golden and set. Transfer to a wire rack to cool before filling.

CRUMB CRUST

This easy crumb crust, popular for cheesecakes, is ideal for chilled tarts since it remains crisp and crunchy, and is particularly good for ice cream tarts and chilled chiffon mixtures. For alternative flavorings to suit different fillings, use vanilla, chocolate, Amaretti cookies (about 24), or gingersnaps (about 24–26 cookies) instead of Graham crackers or replace ½ cup of the crumbs with ½ cup finely chopped nuts for a Nut Crumb Crust.

Ingredients

- For a 9-inch tart pan

- 1½ cups Graham cracker (about 18–20 crackers) or other cookie crumbs
- 6 tbsp butter or margarine, melted
- 1–2 tbsp sugar, or to taste

1 If making your own crumbs, put the Graham crackers or cookies in the bowl of a food processor fitted with the metal blade and process 20–30 seconds until fine crumbs form. Alternatively put them in a heavy-duty freezer bag and press into fine crumbs with a rolling pin. Pour them into a bowl and stir in the melted butter or margarine and sugar, if using. Pour into a tart pan and press crumbs onto the bottom and up the side of tart pan or pie plate. Chill, uncovered, for 20 minutes in the refrigerator.

2 Preheat the oven to 375°F. Bake crust 6–8 minutes until set. Remove to wire rack to cool. It must be completely cool before filling.

CREAM CHEESE PASTRY

Cream Cheese Pastry is a moist, flaky pastry often used with sugary or nutty fillings. It is ideal for rich tartlets and tiny petit fours.

Ingredients

- For a 9-inch tart pan or twelve 2- or 3-inch tartlet pans

- 1 cup all-purpose flour
- ½ tsp salt
- 1 tsp sugar
- ½ cup (1 stick) unsalted butter, at room temperature
- 4 oz full-fat cream cheese, at room temperature

1 In a large bowl, sift together the flour and salt. Add the butter and cream cheese and, with an electric mixer, beat the ingredients together until well-blended and a soft dough forms. Shape into a ball, flatten to a circle and wrap tightly. Refrigerate about 1 hour before rolling and shaping.

RICH CHEESE PASTRY

This pastry is based on a Rich Pie Crust and makes a rich, flavorful alternative pastry for savory tarts. It complements tomato-based fillings. Use a grated hard cheese such as Cheddar or Monterey Jack.

Ingredients

- For a 10-inch tart pan

- 1¼ cups all-purpose flour
- ¼ tsp salt
- ⅛ tsp cayenne pepper

- ½ tsp dry mustard powder
- 6 tbsp cold unsalted butter, cut into small pieces
- 2 tbsp cold white vegetable fat, cut into small pieces
- ½ cup grated sharp Cheddar cheese
- 1 egg yolk beaten with 2 tbsp iced water

Proceed as for Rich Pie Crust, adding the cheese after the butter and white vegetable fat are cut in, and mix well to combine.

CHOCOLATE PASTRY

This is a wonderfully rich, sweet pastry, almost like a chocolate cookie. It makes a stunning background for fruit tarts and tartlets as well as chocolate fillings.

Ingredients
- For a 9- or 10-inch tart pan

- ½ cup (1 stick) unsalted butter, softened
- ⅓ cup superfine sugar
- ½ tsp salt
- 2 tsp vanilla extract
- ½ cup unsweetened cocoa powder (preferably Dutch-processed)
- 1½ cups all-purpose flour

1 Put the butter, sugar, salt, and vanilla into the bowl of a food processor fitted with the metal blade and process 25–30 seconds until creamy, scraping down the sides of the bowl when necessary. Add the cocoa and process about 1 minute, until well blended. Add the flour all at once and, using the pulse button, process 10–15 seconds until the flour is well blended. Scrape dough out onto a sheet of plastic wrap and shape into a flat circle. Wrap and refrigerate.

2 Soften the dough 10–15 minutes at room temperature. Unwrap the dough and sandwich between two large pieces of plastic wrap. Carefully roll out to about an 11-inch round, about ¼-inch thick. Peel off the top sheet and invert the dough into a greased pan. Gently ease the dough onto the bottom and sides of the pan, then remove the bottom layer of plastic wrap. Press the dough onto the bottom and sides of the pan, then roll the rolling pin over the top of the pan to cut off any excess dough. Prick the base of the dough with a fork and refrigerate 1 hour.

3 Preheat the oven to 400°F. Blind bake for 10 minutes. Remove the paper or foil and beans and continue baking 5 minutes more until just set. Transfer to a wire rack to cool completely.

TIPS FOR FILLING TARTS

- For easier handling, and to avoid any overflows, always set tart pan on a heavy baking sheet.
- Beat the eggs and milk or cream mixture in a large measuring cup or pitcher, rather than a bowl, since it will be easier to pour.
- To fill the tart shell with a liquid filling, set the tart on a baking sheet. Pull out the middle oven rack halfway and set the tart on its baking sheet on the rack. Pour in as much filling as possible and gently slide the rack back in place. Bake 5 minutes as this allows a thin crust to form over the top. If any mixture remains, pull the oven rack out and carefully pour the remaining mixture into the center of the tart. Slide the rack back in place.
- To remove the side of the tart pan, set the tart pan bottom on a sturdy can and allow the side to drop down gently onto the surface, leaving the tart on the bottom of the pan. Slide onto a serving plate.
- For a savory tart, sprinkle cheese over the partially baked tart shell to keep the pastry from getting soggy. When the cheese melts it forms a barrier between the pastry and the filling.
- Rubbing an unbaked tart shell with 1 tablespoon of softened butter and chilling before filling helps prevent a soggy crust.
- Brushing a warm, blind-baked tart shell with a little beaten egg or egg white and returning it to the oven for 2 minutes, creates a seal between the pastry and the filling, preventing a soggy crust. Brushing a baked tart shell with melted preserves helps prevent a fruit-filled tart from becoming soggy.
- There are many tart pans on the market. Use a dull metal or non-stick pan as they produce the most well-cooked, crisp pastry. Shiny metal reflects heat, and glass and china absorb it, preventing the pastry from browning well. A trick I use to present or transport a tart is this: bake the tart in a metal, removeable-bottomed pan. Remove the side of the pan from the baked tart, leaving it on the metal bottom, then slide into a quiche dish of the same size.
- To test if the filling is set, insert a sharp knife into the center. It should come out clean and should feel hot to the touch.
- If the pastry edge begins to brown before the filling is set, cover with foil.

chapter two

FROM THE OCEANS
TO THE PRAIRIES

SMOKED SALMON, CREAMY LEEK, AND ORANGE TART

A hint of orange zest brings out the flavor of the leeks and smoked salmon.

● Preheat the oven to 375°F. Put the leeks, whipping cream, and orange zest into a medium saucepan. Set over medium-high heat and bring to a boil. Simmer until the leeks are tender and cream reduced to a thick purée consistency. Remove from the heat and stir in the chives or dill and season with pepper. Spread evenly on the bottom of the tart shell.

● Arrange the smoked salmon strips evenly over the leek mixture. Set on a baking sheet for easier handling.
● Beat the sour cream, egg, and egg yolk and pour over the leeks and smoked salmon strips. Bake until filling is set and golden, about 25 minutes. Transfer to a wire rack to cool slightly. Serve warm or at room temperature.

. . . .
● 9-inch tart pan lined with Rich Pie Crust (*Pâte Brisée Riche*), partially blind-baked

● 3 leeks, trimmed, washed, and cut into ¼-inch slices
● 1 cup whipping cream
● grated zest of ½ orange
● 2 tbsp chopped fresh chives or dill
● freshly ground black pepper
● ½ lb smoked salmon, cut into thin strips
● 3 tbsp sour cream or crème fraîche
● 1 egg
● 1 egg yolk
. . . .

CHEESY HAM AND BROCCOLI TART

- 8 x 12-inch rectangular tart pan lined with Cheese Pastry, partially blind-baked

- 10 oz blanched broccoli flowerets
- 8 oz cooked ham, cut into ½-inch pieces
- 1½ cups whipping cream
- ½ cup milk
- 3 eggs
- 2 egg yolks
- salt
- freshly ground black pepper
- 1 cup grated Gruyère or Emmenthal cheese

The classic flavors of ham and cheese marry well with broccoli.

- Preheat the oven to 375°F. Arrange the blanched broccoli evenly over the bottom of the tart shell, then sprinkle the ham pieces or slices over.

- Beat the cream, milk, eggs, and egg yolks until well blended. Season with salt and pepper and stir in the cheese. Pour over the filling. Bake until set and golden, 30–35 minutes. Transfer to a wire rack to cool slightly. Serve hot or warm.

ROASTED SALMON AND SCALLION TART

- 8-inch square tart pan lined with ½ lb store-bought puff pastry, blind-baked

- 1 lb fresh salmon filet
- 1 tbsp olive oil
- 2 tbsp butter
- 4–6 scallions, cut into 2-inch pieces
- ¼ cup sour cream
- 2 tbsp chopped fresh chives
- salt
- freshly ground black pepper
- 2 tbsp chopped nuts mixed with 1 tbsp dried bread crumbs

This tart can be made with leftover poached salmon, but the oven roasting gives it a more pronounced flavor.

- Preheat the oven to 425°F. Line a small roasting pan with foil. Put the salmon filet in the pan and brush with the oil. Roast until the fish is golden and just opaque, 10–12 minutes. Transfer to a wire rack to cool slightly.
- In a medium skillet over medium-high heat, melt the butter. Add the scallions and cook, stirring frequently, until lightly colored. Stir in the sour cream until blended and season with salt and pepper. Remove from the heat.

- Using a fork, flake the fish into fairly large pieces and stir into the scallion mixture, tossing to blend. Spread in the tart shell and sprinkle with the nut-bread crumb mixture. Return to the oven for 2–3 minutes, until the top is crisp and tart is heated through. Serve immediately.

Right: Cheesy Ham and Broccoli Tart

CRAB AND RED PEPPER TARTLETS

- 4 sheets phyllo dough, defrosted if frozen
- 4–5 tbsp butter, melted
- 3 red bell peppers, seeded and cut lengthwise into thin strips
- 1 tbsp chopped dill
- 4 tbsp freshly grated Parmesan cheese
- ½ lb fresh white crabmeat
- 2 tbsp mayonnaise
- 1 tbsp lemon or lime juice

Buy good quality fresh white crabmeat for these delicate tartlets. Use a mini-muffin pan to make hors d'oeuvre-size tartlets.

- In a large skillet over medium heat, heat 2 tablespoons of the butter. Add the red bell pepper strips and cook until softened, about 10 minutes. Remove from the heat and stir in the dill.
- Preheat the oven to 350°F. Lightly grease eight 2½ x 1¼-inch muffin pan cups. Stack the phyllo dough sheets on a work surface and cut into 4- to 5-inch squares.
- Place one square on the work surface and brush lightly with a little butter; do not brush right up to the edge. Sprinkle with a little Parmesan cheese. Place a second square on top of the first at right angles, to create a star shape. Brush lightly with butter and sprinkle with a little Parmesan. Top with a third square, at an angle to the first two, but do not brush with butter. Ease into one of the muffin pan cups, keeping the edges pointing up to form a flat-bottomed tulip shape. (Keep the phyllo dough sheets covered with a damp dishtowel to prevent dough from drying out.) Line the remaining cups.
- Bake until crisp and golden, about 10 minutes. Transfer to a wire rack to cool slightly. Carefully remove each phyllo shell and set on a wire rack to cool. Divide the pepper mixture evenly among the tartlet shells and top each with a little crabmeat. Mix the mayonnaise with the lemon or lime juice and drizzle a little sauce over the crabmeat. Garnish with dill sprigs. Serve warm or cold.

CREAMY LOBSTER TARTLETS

- 3–4 sheets phyllo dough, defrosted if frozen
- 3–4 tbsp butter, melted
- 4 tbsp freshly grated Parmesan cheese
- 1½ lb cooked fresh lobster meat
- 1 cup whipping cream
- 1 egg
- 1 egg yolk
- salt
- pinch of cayenne pepper
- freshly grated nutmeg

This is an extravagant dish as it requires a good portion of lobster for each serving.

- Preheat the oven to 375°F. Lightly grease six 3-inch tartlet pans. Cut 24 4-inch circles from the phyllo dough.
- Place one circle on the work surface and brush lightly with a little butter. Ease into one of the tartlet pans. Sprinkle with a little Parmesan cheese. Brush a second circle with a little of the butter and layer over the first, sprinkle with a little cheese and top with a third dough round. Keep the remaining phyllo dough circles covered with a damp dishtowel to prevent the dough from drying out. Line the remaining tartlet pans.
- Divide the lobster meat evenly among the lined tartlet shells. Beat the cream, egg, and egg yolk until well blended. Season with salt, cayenne pepper, and freshly grated nutmeg. Divide evenly among the tartlet shells and sprinkle each with any remaining cheese. Bake until the filling is set and the pastry crisp, about 15 minutes. Cool slightly and then serve.

Right: Crab and Red Pepper Tartlets

SEAFOOD AND TOMATO CREAM TART

- 9-inch tart pan lined with Rich Pie Crust (*Pâte Brisée Riche*), partially blind-baked

- 1 tbsp butter
- 1 small onion, chopped
- 4 plum tomatoes, peeled, seeded, and chopped
- 1 tbsp all-purpose flour
- ½ tsp dried thyme
- 1 tbsp tomato paste
- 1½ cups whipping cream
- salt
- freshly ground black pepper
- 1 tbsp fresh parsley, chopped
- 1 lb cooked mixed seafood or medium shrimp, well-drained
- 2 eggs

This creamy tomato-flavored custard makes a perfect base for shrimp, or lobster, as well as mixed seafood.

● Preheat the oven to 375°F. In a medium saucepan over medium heat, melt the butter. Add the onion and cook until just softened, 3–5 minutes. Stir in the chopped tomatoes, sprinkle in the flour and cook 1–2 minutes more.
● Add the thyme and tomato paste and whisk in the cream. Cook, stirring frequently, until the sauce is thickened and reduced by about one third. Season with salt and pepper and stir in the parsley. Remove from the heat to cool slightly.
● Spread the seafood evenly on the bottom of the tart shell. Set on a baking sheet for easier handling. Beat the eggs into the tomato cream and pour over the seafood. Bake until set and golden, about 35 minutes. Transfer to a wire rack to cool slightly. Serve warm or at room temperature.

PROSCIUTTO, FIG, AND FONTINA BARQUETTES

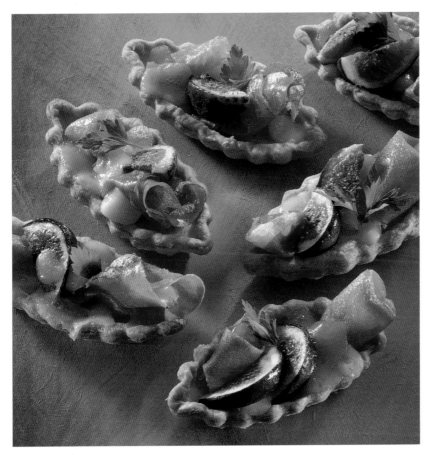

The saltiness of the prosciutto and sweetness of the figs are balanced by the fontina cheese to create a delicious little pastry hors d'oeuvre. If you like, use to fill six 3-inch tartlets and serve as a starter.

. . . .

- 12 barquette molds lined with Rich Pie Crust (*Pâte Brisée Riche*), blind-baked

- 12 slices prosciutto (Parma ham), trimmed, cut in half lengthwise
  - 4 figs, halved and thinly sliced
  - 1 cup diced fontina cheese
  - freshly ground black pepper
  - parsley or basil leaves for garnish

. . . .

● Preheat the oven to 375°F. Roll the prosciutto and fill the barquettes with fig slices and diced cheese and prosciutto rolls. Grind a little black pepper over each tartlet. Set on a baking sheet for easier handling.

● Bake until the cheese is just melted and pastry heated through, about 3–5 minutes. Serve hot or warm.

SPANISH TORTILLA TART

....
• 9-inch deep tart pan lined with Rich Pie Crust
(*Pâte Brisée Riche*), partially blind-baked

• 1 tbsp olive oil
• 1 small onion, thinly sliced
• 1 red or green bell pepper, seeded and thinly sliced
• 2 garlic cloves, chopped
• 2–3 sun-dried tomatoes, packed in oil, chopped
• 8–10 pitted black olives, chopped
• 1 large potato (about 8 oz), cooked and sliced
• 2 oz chorizo, cut into thin strips
• 2 tsp chopped canned jalapeño chiles
• 4 eggs
• ¾ cups milk
• ¼ cup whipping cream
• ½ tsp salt
• freshly ground black pepper
• ½ tsp paprika
• ⅔ cup grated Monterey Jack or Cheddar cheese
....

The pastry shell creates a tender, flaky case for an omelet-like filling with typical Spanish-style flavors.

• Preheat the oven to 375°F. In a medium skillet over medium heat, heat the oil. Add the onion, bell pepper, and garlic and cook, stirring occasionally, until softened, about 8 minutes. Reserve one quarter of the mixture and spread the remainder evenly on the bottom of the tart shell. Set on a baking sheet for easier handling.
• Sprinkle the onion mixture with three-quarters of the sun-dried tomatoes and olives, and arrange the potato slices over the top. Sprinkle over the remaining onion-pepper mixture, sun-dried tomatoes, and olives.

• Beat the eggs and milk. Season with salt, pepper, and the paprika, then stir in the cheese. Pour over the vegetable layers. Bake until set and golden, about 30 minutes. Transfer to a wire rack to cool slightly. Serve hot, warm, or at room temperature.

QUICHE LORRAINE

....
• 9-inch tart pan lined with Rich Pie Crust (*Pâte Brisée Riche*), partially blind-baked

• ½ lb bacon, cut into ¼-inch slices
• 1½ cups whipping cream
• 3 eggs
• 1 egg yolk
• ½ tsp salt
• freshly ground black pepper
• freshly grated nutmeg
....

The authentic "Quiche," which originates in the Lorraine region of France, is a custard-based tart containing bacon, cream, and eggs, and is served as an hors d'oeuvre. Purists say only this tart can be called a quiche. If you like, add 1 cup grated Gruyère to the custard mixture.

• Preheat the oven to 375°F. Set the blind-baked tart shell on a baking sheet for easier handling.

• Put the sliced bacon in a skillet set over low heat. When the fat begins to melt, increase the heat to medium and fry, stirring occasionally, until crisp. Drain on paper towels and sprinkle over the bottom of the tart shell.
• Beat the eggs, milk, and cream. Season with salt, pepper, and the paprika, then stir in the cheese. Pour over the vegetable layers. Bake until set and golden, about 30 minutes. Transfer to a wire rack to cool slightly. Serve hot, warm, or at room temperature.

Right: Spanish Tortilla Tart

PEPPERONI, TOMATO, AND CHEESE GALETTE

. . . .
- ¾ lb store-bought puff pastry or Rich Pie Crust (Pâte Brisée Riche)

- 1 tbsp virgin olive oil, plus extra for drizzling
- 1 small onion, chopped
- 2 garlic cloves
- 1 x 14-oz can Italian-style tomatoes
- 1 tbsp tomato paste
- 1 tsp dried oregano
- salt
- freshly ground black pepper
- 4 oz thinly sliced pepperoni
- 1 cup grated Mozzarella cheese
- fresh oregano leaves for sprinkling and extra for garnish
- 3 tbsp freshly grated Parmesan cheese
. . . .

Use store-bought puff-pastry or Rich Pie Crust for this tasty pizza-like tart.

- On a lightly floured surface, roll out the pastry to make a 10- or 11-inch circle. Carefully slide the circle onto a lightly floured baking sheet and prick the bottom all over. Refrigerate ½ hour.
- In a medium skillet over medium-high heat, heat the oil. Add the onion and cook, stirring occasionally, until beginning to soften, about 3 minutes. Add the garlic and cook 1 minute more. Stir in the tomatoes, tomato paste, and dried oregano. Cook until the sauce is thickened and reduced, about 10–12 minutes. Season with salt and pepper. Remove from the heat to cool slightly.

- Preheat the oven to 400°F. Wrap a 10-inch dinner plate with foil and center it over the pastry. Weight it with baking beans and blind-bake for 10 minutes, turning the shell halfway through the cooking time. Remove the weights and plate and bake for 2 minutes more.
- Spread the cooled tomato sauce evenly over the pastry circle to within ½ inch of the edge. Arrange the pepperoni slices evenly over the top, sprinkle with the mozzarella and a few oregano leaves. Spoon over the Parmesan cheese. Bake until the pastry is crisp and cheese is browned and bubbling, about 10 minutes. (If the top browns too quickly, cover with foil.)

JUMBO SHRIMP AND FENNEL TARTLETS

. . . .
- Six 3-inch tartlet pans lined with Rich Pie Crust (Pâte Brisée Riche), blind-baked

- 2 tbsp butter
- 2 large fennel bulbs, trimmed, quartered and thinly sliced
- 4 tbsp whipping cream
- 1 tbsp Pernod or anise-flavored liqueur
- salt
- cayenne pepper
- 18 jumbo shrimp, peeled and deveined
- 3 tbsp freshly grated Parmesan cheese
- dill sprigs for garnish
. . . .

The slight anise flavor of the fennel goes well with most seafood. The Pernod is not essential but does enhance the flavor even more.

- Preheat the oven to 375°F. In a medium skillet over medium heat, melt 1 tablespoon of the butter. Add the fennel and cook, stirring occasionally, until fennel is tender. Stir in 2 tablespoons of the whipping cream, add the Pernod and season with the salt and cayenne. Cook 2–3 minutes more until the fennel is glazed and the cream absorbed. Divide the mixture evenly between the tartlet shells. Set them on a baking sheet for easier handling.

- Add the remaining butter to the skillet. Add the shrimp and the remaining cream, and stir gently until coated and heated through.
- Arrange three shrimp on each of the tartlet shells and sprinkle each with a little cheese. Bake 5–7 minutes until the shrimp are glazed and tartlets crisp and heated through. Garnish and serve immediately.

Right: Pepperoni, Tomato, and Cheese Galette

chapter three
VEGETABLE TARTS

SWEET GARLIC, THYME, AND OLIVE TART

This strong-flavored tart is served with goat cheese and basil on top — it makes a great talking point. Substitute arugula or watercress for basil if you like and try it with other savory tarts.

● In a small saucepan over low heat, melt the butter. Add the garlic and thyme and cook, covered, 15–20 minutes, stirring occasionally, until the garlic is soft. Remove from the heat to cool slightly. Squeeze the garlic from its skin and discard skins. Mash the pulp with the butter and thyme.

● Preheat the oven to 375°F. In a medium skillet, heat 1 tablespoon of the olive oil.

Add the onion and cook, stirring frequently, until soft and translucent, about 10 minutes. Spread evenly over the bottom of the tart shell.

● Beat the cream and eggs and stir in the garlic purée. Pour into the onion-filled tart shell and sprinkle the olives over the top. Bake until just set and lightly colored, about 30 minutes. Remove to a wire rack to cool slightly.

● In a small bowl, toss the diced feta cheese in the remaining olive oil with the chile flakes. Arrange on the warm tart with the basil leaves or watercress or arugula. Serve immediately.

. . . .

● 8- or 9-inch tart pan lined with Rich Pie Crust (*Pâte Brisée Riche*), partially blind-baked

● 2 tbsp butter
● 4–6 large young garlic cloves, unpeeled
● 2 tsp fresh thyme leaves, chopped, or 1 tsp dried thyme
● 2 tbsp extra-virgin olive oil
● 1 large sweet onion, thinly sliced
● 1 cup whipping cream
● 2 eggs
● 1 cup mixed good quality black and green olives, rinsed, pitted, and halved
● 2 oz feta cheese, diced
● ⅛ tsp chile flakes
● handful fresh basil leaves or watercress or arugula

. . . .

FANCY ASPARAGUS TRANCHE

- 14 x 4-inch tart pan lined with Cheese Pie Crust or Rich Pie Crust, partially blind-baked

- 1 tbsp butter
- 1 lb thin asparagus tips, well washed
- ½ cup half-and-half
- 2 eggs
- 1 egg yolk
- ½ tsp salt
- ¼ tsp cayenne pepper
- 3 tbsp freshly chopped dill or chives
- 2 tsp Dijon-style mustard

A tranche is a "slice" in French. This rectangular tart makes an elegant presentation as well as being easy to slice.

● Preheat the oven to 350°F. Set the tart shell on a baking sheet for easier handling. In a large skillet over medium-high heat, melt the butter. Add the asparagus tips and cook, tossing gently until tender-crisp and brightly colored, 1–2 minutes. Remove from the heat and cool slightly. Arrange the asparagus spears crosswise and top to tail in the tart shell.

● Beat the half-and-half, eggs, and egg yolk until well blended. Season with salt and cayenne pepper, then stir in the dill or chives and mustard. Pour into the tart shell. Bake until set and golden, about 25 minutes. Transfer to a wire rack to cool slightly. Serve hot or warm.

CHERRY TOMATO AND BASIL TARTLETS

- Six 4-inch tartlet pans lined with Rich Pie Crust (*Pâte Brisée Riche*), blind-baked

- 24 cherry tomatoes
- 6–8 fresh basil leaves, shredded
- 3 eggs
- 1¼ cups whipping cream
- salt
- freshly ground black pepper
- ½ cup grated Gruyère cheese
- 1 tbsp fresh or bottled pesto sauce

Using fresh or bottled pesto sauce brings out the flavor of these easy-to-assemble tartlets.

● Preheat the oven to 350°F. Arrange the tartlets on a baking sheet for easier handling. Arrange eight cherry tomato halves, cut-side up, in each of the tartlet shells. Sprinkle evenly with the shredded basil leaves.

● Beat the eggs and cream until well blended. Season with salt and pepper and stir in the cheese and pesto sauce. Fill each of the tartlets. Bake until just set and golden, 25 minutes. Transfer the tartlets to a wire rack to cool. Serve warm and garnish with fresh basil leaves.

Right: Fancy Asparagus Tranche

RED ONION TARTE TATIN

- ½ lb store-bought puff pastry or Rich Pie Crust (Pâte Brisée Riche)

- 1 tbsp butter
- 1 tbsp olive oil
- 1½ lbs red onions, halved lengthwise
- ½ tsp dried thyme
- 1 tbsp brown sugar
- ½ tsp salt
- freshly ground black pepper
- ¼ cup water
- 1 tbsp balsamic vinegar

This savory onion tart is based on the famous French Tarte Tatin.

● On a lightly floured surface, roll out the dough to a circle about 10 inches and slightly thicker than ¼ inch. Carefully slide onto a floured baking sheet and refrigerate.

● In a 9-inch ovenproof skillet or flameproof casserole over medium-high heat, melt the butter with the olive oil. Add the onion halves cut side down. Fill any spaces with extra chopped onion. Sprinkle with the thyme, brown sugar, salt and season with the pepper. Cook, shaking the pan occasionally, until the onions begin to color, 3–5 minutes.

● Preheat the oven to 425°F. Add the water and vinegar to the pan and reduce the heat to medium. Cook until the liquid has evaporated and onions are tender-crisp, about 5 minutes. Remove from the heat and cool slightly, 2–3 minutes.

● Slide the rolled-out dough circle over the onion-filled skillet. Using a knife, carefully tuck the dough inside the edge of the pan. Pierce in two or three places. Bake 25–30 minutes until the pastry is crisp and golden.

● Transfer to a wire rack to cool. Run a knife around the edge of the pan. Place a serving plate over the skillet and, using potholders, carefully invert them. Remove the skillet.

SPINACH, CAMEMBERT, AND PINE NUT SQUARE

- 10-inch square tart pan lined with Rich Pie Crust *(Pâte Brisée Riche)*, blind-baked

- 2 tbsp butter
- 2 shallots, finely chopped
- ½ lb baby spinach leaves, washed and dried
- 6 oz Camembert, brie, or other semi-soft cheese, rind removed and cut into small pieces
- ¾ cup sour cream
- 2 eggs
- salt
- freshly grated nutmeg
- 2 tbsp pine nuts

The Camembert and sour cream combine to create a rich creamy filling in this attractive tart.

- Preheat the oven to 350°F. Place the tart shell on a baking sheet for easier handling. In a medium skillet over medium heat, melt 1 tablespoon butter. Add the shallots and cook, stirring often, until just softened, 3–5 minutes. Spread evenly over the bottom of the tart shell.

- Melt the remaining butter in the same skillet and add the spinach, stirring gently, until it wilts, about 1 minute. Spread over the bottom of the tart shell and sprinkle the cut-up cheese over the spinach.
- Beat the sour cream and eggs until well-blended. Season with salt and nutmeg and pour into the tart shell. Sprinkle the pine nuts over the top. Bake until set and golden, 20–25 minutes. Transfer to a wire rack to cool slightly; serve immediately.

ARTICHOKE, ARUGULA, AND CAPER TART

. . . .
- 10-inch tart pan lined with ¾ lb bought puff pastry, partially blind-baked

- 2 tbsp butter or olive oil
- 2 oz fresh arugula
- 1 x 14-oz can artichoke hearts, halved
- ½ tsp dried thyme
- salt
- freshly ground black pepper
- 2 tbsp capers
- 2 tbsp raisins
- 1 cup half-and-half
- 2 eggs
- 1 egg yolk
- ⅓ cup grated fontina or Gruyère cheese
- 2 tbsp chopped hazelnuts (filberts) (optional)

This tart uses bought puff pastry, but could be made with other pie crust doughs or even phyllo pastry.

- Preheat the oven to 375°F. In a large skillet over medium-high heat, melt 1 tablespoon butter or oil. Add the arugula and stir fry until just wilted, about 1 minute. Spread evenly in the bottom of the tart shell.
- Add the remaining butter or oil to the pan and stir in the artichoke halves. Sprinkle with the thyme and season with salt and pepper. Stir gently until just warmed through and seasoned, about 1 minute.
- Arrange the artichoke halves in an attractive pattern, cut side up, over the arugula. Sprinkle the capers and raisins evenly around the artichoke halves.
- Beat the half and half with the eggs and egg yolk if using. Season with salt and pepper and stir in the cheese and chopped nuts. Pour over the vegetables. Bake until set and golden, about 30 minutes. Transfer to a wire rack to cool slightly. Serve warm.

CHEESE SOUFFLÉ TART

. . . .
- 9-inch tart pan lined with Rich Pie Crust (*Pâte Brisée Riche*), partially blind-baked

- 2 tbsp freshly grated Parmesan cheese
- 4 tbsp butter
- 1 small onion, finely chopped
- 4 tbsp flour
- 1¼ cups milk
- 2 eggs, separated
- 1 tbsp Dijon-style mustard
- 1 cup grated Cheddar cheese
- salt
- cayenne pepper
- 1 egg white

. . . .

This cheese soufflé in a pastry case makes a great supper. For a special presentation, make individual tartlets but bake 10 minutes less.

- Sprinkle the tart shell with Parmesan cheese. Set on a baking sheet for easier handling.
- In a medium saucepan over medium heat, melt the butter. Stir in the onion and cook 1–2 minutes. Stir in the flour all at once and cook, stirring constantly, 2 minutes. Gradually whisk in the milk, stirring until thick and smooth. Bring to a boil and cook 1 minute. Remove from the heat. Beat in the egg yolks, one at a time, then beat in the mustard and cheese. Season with a little salt and cayenne pepper. Set aside.
- Preheat the oven to 425°F. In a medium bowl, with an electric mixer, beat all the egg whites with a pinch of salt until soft peaks form. Stir a spoonful of the whites into the cheese sauce to lighten it, then gently fold in the remaining whites and spoon the mixture into the tart shell.
- Bake until the soufflé is puffed and golden, about 25 minutes. Serve immediately as you would a regular soufflé.

Right: Artichoke, Arugula, and Caper Tart

SPICY MEXICALI TART

· · · · · · ·

- 9-inch tart pan lined with Rich Pie Crust *(Pâte Brisée Riche)* or Cheese Pastry

- 1 tbsp vegetable oil
- 2 onions, thinly sliced
- 1 small red bell pepper, seeded and thinly sliced
- 1 garlic clove, finely chopped
- 1 x 7-oz can corn kernels, drained
- 1–2 chopped canned jalapeño chiles
- 1¼ cups milk
- 4 eggs
- salt
- ½ tsp ground cumin
- ¼ cup shredded Monterey Jack
- 2 scallions, finely chopped
- 1 tbsp freshly chopped cilantro

· · · · · · ·

The chopped chiles and Monterey Jack cheese give this tangy tart a Tex-Mex flavor. Adjust the amount of chilies to your own taste.

● In a large skillet over medium heat, heat the oil. Add the onions, red bell pepper, and garlic and cook, stirring occasionally, until softened, 7–10 minutes. Remove from heat. Stir in the corn kernels and chopped chiles and spread evenly in the bottom of the tart shell. Set on a baking sheet for easier handling.

● Preheat the oven to 375°F. Beat the milk and eggs until well blended. Season with salt and the cumin. Stir in the cheese, scallions, and cilantro and pour over the onion mixture. Bake until puffed and golden, about 35 minutes. Transfer to a wire rack to cool slightly. Serve immediately.

CREAMY POTATO TART

· · · · · · ·

- 9-inch tart pan lined with Rich Pie Crust *(Pâte Brisée Riche)*, Cheese Pastry, or Herb Pie Crust, partially blind-baked

- 4 large baking potatoes, unpeeled
- 2 tbsp butter, softened
- salt
- freshly ground black pepper
- ½ tsp dried thyme
- ½ tsp freshly chopped rosemary
- ¾ cup whipping cream
- freshly grated nutmeg

· · · · · · ·

This potato tart makes an unusual accompaniment to roasted meats.

● Put the potatoes in a large saucepan with enough cold water to cover. Bring to a boil over medium-high heat. Reduce the heat and simmer until potatoes are tender. Cool under running cold water for about 5 minutes, then allow to cool completely.

● Preheat the oven to 375°F. Set the tart shell on a baking sheet for easier handling. Peel the potatoes and carefully cut into very thin slices. Arrange a layer of overlapping potato slices on the bottom of the tart shell and dot with a little softened butter. Sprinkle with salt and pepper. Continue layering with the potatoes and butter, and seasoning.

● Stir the herbs into the cream and season with a little more salt, pepper, and grated nutmeg. Pour the cream over the potato layers, allowing it to seep between each layer. The cream should just come up to the top layer. Dot with butter.

● Bake tart until the cream is absorbed and the top is golden and crisp, about 30 minutes. Transfer to a wire rack to cool slightly.

Right: Spicy Mexicali Tart

CHAR-BROILED EGGPLANT AND PEPPER TART

- 9-inch tart pan lined with Rich Pie Crust *(Pâte Brisée Riche)* or Cheese Pastry, partially blind-baked

- 1 medium eggplant, thinly sliced crosswise
- 2 zucchini, sliced diagonally crosswise
- ¼ cup olive oil
- 1 red bell pepper, quartered and seeded
- 1 yellow bell pepper, quartered and seeded
- 1 large red onion, thickly sliced
- 4 oz soft goat cheese, crumbled
- ½ cup whipping cream
- 1 egg
- 1 egg yolk
- 2 tbsp freshly grated Parmesan cheese
- ½ tsp dried oregano
- 1 tbsp tomato paste
- ¼ tsp chile flakes

Broiling the vegetables before baking them in the tart really intensifies the flavors and brings out their sweetness.

- Preheat the broiler. Line the broiler pan with foil and arrange the eggplant and zucchini slices in a single layer on the foil. Brush the surfaces generously with some of the olive oil. Broil the vegetables until just beginning to char, about 5 minutes. Turn and broil 5 minutes more. Arrange on the bottom of the tart shell. Set on a baking sheet for easier handling.
- Arrange the red and yellow bell pepper quarters, skin-side up, with the onion rings on the foil and brush with the remaining oil. Broil until just beginning to char, 6–7 minutes. Remove any loosened skin and arrange them over the other vegetables in the tart shell, distributing them evenly. Sprinkle the crumbled goat cheese over the vegetables.
- Preheat the oven to 400°F. Beat the cream with the egg and egg yolk. Stir in the Parmesan cheese, oregano, tomato paste, and chile flakes until well-blended. Pour over the vegetables in the tart shell. Bake until the filling is set and top is well colored, about 25 minutes. Transfer to a wire rack to cool slightly. Serve warm.

TOMATO, MOZZARELLA, AND PESTO TARTLETS

- Six 3-inch tartlet pans lined with Rich Pie Crust *(Pâte Brisée Riche)*, blind-baked

- 4 tbsp fresh or bottled pesto sauce
- 6 oz mozzarella cheese, sliced
- 4–6 small Italian-style plum tomatoes, thinly sliced
- about 24 basil leaves
- 1 tbsp pine nuts

This combination of sweet-sharp tomatoes and creamy mozzarella is enhanced by a zingy pesto sauce.

- Preheat the oven to 400°F. Spread the bottom of each tartlet shell with a little pesto sauce. Arrange alternate slices of the cheese and tomato in an overlapping circle, tucking in 3–4 basil leaves between them. Sprinkle with a few pine nuts.
- Set the tartlet shells on a baking sheet for easier handling. Bake until the cheese is softened and pine nuts just golden, 8–10 minutes. Serve immediately.

Right: Charbroiled Eggplant and Pepper Tart

RED ONION AND BLACK OLIVE TARTLETS

- Six 3-inch tartlet pans lined with Rich Pie Crust (*Pâte Brisée Riche*), blind-baked

- 6 tbsp Parmesan cheese, freshly grated
- 2–3 tbsp olive oil
- 4–5 large young garlic cloves, unpeeled
- 2 tbsp butter
- 3 red onions, thinly sliced
- ½ tsp dried thyme
- 2 tbsp whipping cream
- 1 tbsp fresh parsley, chopped
- 18–24 good quality black olives, such as Kalamata, pitted and halved

The slight saltiness of the black olives makes a perfect contrast with the sweetness of the slowly cooked onions and garlic.

- Sprinkle each tartlet shell with a tablespoon of Parmesan cheese. Set on a baking sheet for easier handling.
- In a small saucepan over low heat, heat the olive oil. Add the garlic and cook, covered, 15–20 minutes, stirring frequently, until the garlic is soft. Remove from the heat and squeeze the garlic from their skins into a small bowl, mashing to blend.

- Preheat the oven to 375°F. Meanwhile, melt the butter in a medium skillet over medium heat. Add the onions and cook, stirring frequently, until soft and translucent, about 10 minutes. Stir in the dried thyme and cream, and cook 3–5 minutes more until all the liquid is absorbed and the onions are a purée-like consistency. Stir in the chopped parsley and reserved garlic purée.
- Carefully divide the onion mixture among the tartlet shells and sprinkle with the black olives. Bake until just heated through, about 5 minutes. Serve warm.

GORGONZOLA, PEAR, AND PECAN TARTLETS

- Six 3-inch tartlet pans, lined with Rich Pie Crust (*Pâte Brisée Riche*), enriched with ¼ cup chopped pecans or walnuts, blind-baked

- 1 tbsp butter
- 2 medium dessert pears, peeled, cored, and diced
- ¼ tsp dried thyme
- 1 shallot, finely chopped
- 6 oz Gorgonzola or other creamy blue cheese, crumbled
- ½ cup coarsely chopped pecans or walnuts
- ⅔ cup whipping cream
- 2 eggs
- pinch of cayenne pepper
- freshly grated nutmeg

This may seem an unlikely combination but the contrasting flavors provide a delicious result.

- Preheat the oven to 375°F. Set the tartlet shells on a baking sheet for easier handling.
- In a medium skillet over medium-high heat, melt the butter. Add the pears and stir fry until well coated with the butter, about 1–2 minutes. Sprinkle in the thyme and shallot and toss well, cook 1 minute more. Divide the mixture evenly among the tartlet shells, distributing the pieces evenly on the bottom of each.
- Distribute the cheese among the tartlet shells, spreading evenly. Sprinkle each with the chopped pecans or walnuts.
- Beat the cream and eggs until well blended and season with cayenne pepper and freshly grated nutmeg. Divide the mixture evenly among the tartlets. Bake until tops are golden and the cheese melted, about 10 minutes. Transfer to a wire rack to cool slightly. Serve hot or warm.

SUN-DRIED TOMATO AND MOZZARELLA TART

- 1 recipe Rich Pie Crust (Pâte Brisée Riche)

- ¾ cup homemade thick tomato sauce or store-bought pizza topping
- 8 oz mozzarella cheese, shredded
- 4–5 large Italian-style plum tomatoes, sliced
- 6 sun-dried tomatoes, packed in oil, drained and sliced
- 8 oz smoked mozzarella, sliced
- 6–8 fresh basil leaves, torn into small pieces plus extra for garnish
- virgin olive oil for drizzling
- freshly ground black pepper

Transform the idea of the classic tomato and cheese pizza by updating the ingredients and arranging them on a pastry base.

● Preheat the oven to 400°F. Roll out the pastry to an 11-inch circle and use to line a 10-inch lightly greased pizza tray or shallow tart pan. Prick the bottom and blind bake for 10 minutes.

● Remove from the oven and prick the bottom again. Immediately spread the bottom evenly with the tomato sauce or pizza topping and sprinkle with the grated cheese. Return to the oven until the cheese just begins to melt, 3–5 minutes. Remove from the oven and cool slightly.

● Arrange the sliced tomatoes, sun-dried tomatoes, and smoked mozzarella overlapping on the surface of the tart shell in a decorative pattern. Sprinkle with the torn basil. Drizzle with about 1 tablespoon of olive oil and season with the pepper.

● Return to the oven until the pastry is golden and the cheese melted, and just beginning to color, about 8 minutes. Serve, hot, drizzled with additional olive oil and garnish with fresh basil leaves.

YELLOW SQUASH AND PROVOLONE TART

- 9-inch tart pan lined with Rich Pie Crust (Pâte Brisée Riche), blind-baked

- 1 tbsp olive oil
- 1 tbsp butter
- 10 oz yellow squash or zucchini, diced
- 1 small red bell pepper, diced
- ½ tsp salt
- freshly ground black pepper
- 2 tbsp bottled pesto sauce
- 1 cup half-and-half
- 2 eggs
- ½ cup grated Provolone cheese, preferably aged

If yellow squash is hard to find or out of season, simply use young zucchini.

● Preheat the oven to 375°F. Set the tart shell on a baking sheet for easier handling.

● In a large skillet over medium-high heat, heat the oil and butter. Add the yellow squash or zucchini and red bell pepper and cook, stirring frequently, until just beginning to soften, about 5 minutes. Season with salt and pepper and spread onto the bottom of the tart shell. Drizzle with the pesto sauce.

● Beat the half-and-half and eggs until blended. Stir in the grated cheese and pour over the filled tart shell. Bake until set and golden, about 35 minutes. Transfer to a wire rack to cool slightly. Serve hot or warm.

Right: Sun-dried Tomato and Mozzarella Tart

RED PEPPER AND ZUCCHINI RIBBON TART

- 9-inch tart pan lined with Rich Pie Crust (*Pâte Brisée Riche*) or Cheese Pastry, partially blind-baked

- 2 tbsp butter
- 1 tbsp olive oil
- 2 large red bell peppers, seeded and diced
- 1 plum tomato, seeded and chopped
- 1 tsp sugar
- salt
- freshly ground black pepper
- 4 medium zucchini, washed, dried and trimmed
- 1 cup milk
- 2 eggs
- ½ cup grated Monterey Jack or Cheddar cheese
- ½ tsp salt
- freshly grated nutmeg

This tart makes an ideal light lunch and can be made with other sweet peppers such as yellow or orange. Use yellow squash when in season.

● In a medium skillet over medium heat, melt 1 tablespoon of the butter and the olive oil. Add the bell peppers and tomato and cook, stirring occasionally, until softened and any liquid is evaporated, 10–12 minutes. Stir in the sugar and season with salt and pepper. Spread the mixture evenly onto the bottom of the tart shell.

● Preheat the oven to 350°F. Using a swivel-bladed vegetable peeler, peel each zucchini lengthwise into "ribbons." In a large skillet, melt the remaining butter over medium-high heat. Add the zucchini ribbons and toss, stirring, until they just begin to soften, about 1 minute. Remove from the heat to cool slightly. Arrange the ribbons over the bell pepper mixture.
● Beat the milk, eggs, and cheese and season with the salt, pepper, and a little grated nutmeg. Pour into the tart shell. Bake until the filling is set and the pastry golden, about 25 minutes. Transfer to a wire rack to cool slightly. Serve hot, warm, or cold.

BROCCOLI, CREAM CHEESE, AND PINE NUT TART

- 9-inch tart pan lined with Light Whole-wheat Pie Crust, partially blind-baked

- ½ lb broccoli flowerets
- 6 oz cream cheese or soft cheese with garlic and herbs, softened
- ¾ cup half-and-half
- 3 eggs
- 1 egg yolk
- salt
- freshly ground black pepper
- 4 scallions, finely chopped
- 1–2 tbsp freshly chopped parsley or dill
- 2 tbsp pine nuts

For a hint of garlic and herbs, replace the cream cheese with a soft cheese with garlic and herbs, or add your own.

● Preheat the oven to 375°F. Bring a medium saucepan half filled with water to a boil. Drop in the broccoli and bring back to a boil, cook 3–4 minutes. Drain and rinse under running cold water; drain and pat dry. Arrange broccoli evenly over the bottom of the tart shell. Set on a baking sheet for easier handling.

● Beat the cream cheese or soft cheese until smooth. Gradually beat in the half-and-half, eggs, and egg yolk. Season with salt and pepper. Stir in the scallions and parsley or dill and pour into the tart shell.
● Sprinkle the pine nuts over the top. Bake until set and golden, about 35 minutes. Transfer to a wire rack to cool slightly. Serve warm.

Right: Red Pepper and Zucchini Ribbon Tart

RUSTIC STRAWBERRY RHUBARB TART

The classic strawberry-rhubarb combination is an ideal filling for an easy-to-make tart. It is also excellent made with apples and blackberries.

● Lightly spray or oil a large baking sheet. On a lightly floured surface, roll out the pastry to a 13- or 14-inch circle, it doesn't matter if the shape is not perfect or if the edges tear, this is a rustic tart. Slide onto the baking sheet and refrigerate 30 minutes.
● In a large skillet over high heat, melt the butter. Add the rhubarb and stir fry until the juices begin to run and it just begins to lose its color. Sprinkle in 3–4 tbsp sugar and the flour and toss to coat. Remove from the heat and add the strawberries, tossing lightly to combine. Cool about 5 minutes.

● Preheat the oven to 400°F. Remove the dough circle from the refrigerator to soften, about 5 minutes. Sprinkle the surface of the dough with the toasted or dried bread crumbs and spoon the fruit onto the dough to within 3–4 inches of the border.
● Using your fingertips, fold and crimp the wide border of the dough over the fruit toward the center. Sprinkle with a little sugar. It doesn't matter if pastry cracks or is uneven, just pinch it together. Bake until the pastry is crisp and golden and fruit is bubbling, 35–40 minutes. Transfer the tart on its baking sheet to a wire rack to cool slightly. Serve hot or warm.

. . . .

● 1 recipe Basic Sweet Crust *(Pâte Sucrée)* or Extra Sweet Tart Crust *(Pâte Sucrée Riche)*

● 1 tbsp butter
● 1 lb rhubarb, cut into 1-inch pieces
● sugar
● 2 tbsp all-purpose flour
● 1 lb strawberries, hulled and halved if large
● ¼ cup fresh bread crumbs, toasted or homemade dried bread crumbs

. . . .

CHOCOLATE BANOFFEE TART

- 9-inch deep tart pan lined with Chocolate Pastry or Chocolate or Ginger Crumb Crust, blind-baked

- 2 x 14-oz cans sweetened condensed milk
- 6 oz bittersweet chocolate, chopped
- ⅔ cup whipping cream
- 1 tbsp light corn syrup
- 3 ripe bananas

WHITE CHOCOLATE WHIPPED CREAM
- 1¾ cups whipping cream
- 5 oz good quality white chocolate, grated
- ½ tsp vanilla extract
- unsweetened cocoa powder, for dusting

Banoffee pie is an all-time favorite. Covering it with white chocolate whipped cream sends it right over the top. The toffee layer can be done ahead, but don't add the bananas and cream more than a few hours before serving.

- Using an old-fashioned can opener, puncture each of the cans of milk (this prevents any possible explosion while cooking). Put them in a medium saucepan and add enough water to cover. Bring to a boil over medium-high heat. Reduce the heat and simmer, covered, about 2 hours. Be sure to top up with water (some milk may leak but this does not matter). Carefully remove tins from water and cool.
- In a medium saucepan over medium-low heat, combine the chocolate, cream, corn syrup, and butter. Cook until smooth and melted, stirring constantly. Pour into the prepared crust and refrigerate until set, about 1 hour.

- Prepare the white chocolate whipped cream. In a small saucepan over medium heat, bring ½ cup of the cream to a boil. Remove from the heat and stir in the grated white chocolate all at once, continue stirring until completely smooth. Stir in the vanilla extract. Strain into a medium bowl and cool to room temperature.
- Scrape the condensed milk into a bowl. Whisk the thickened "toffee" until smooth. Immediately spread evenly over the chocolate layer in the tart shell.
- Slice the bananas thinly and arrange them in overlapping concentric circles over the toffee layer in the tart shell. In a medium bowl, whisk the remaining cream until stiff peaks form. Fold a spoonful into the white chocolate cream to lighten it, then fold in the remaining cream. Spoon over the banana layer and spread to the edge. Dust the top with cocoa if you like. Refrigerate until ready to serve.

LAVENDER-SCENTED APPLE TART

• 10-inch tart pan lined with Basic Sweet Crust
(Pâte Sucrée)

• 4 large Empire, Gala or Golden Delicious apples
• ½ cup Pineaux des Charentes or other sweet
dessert wine
• 3 tbsp granulated sugar
GLAZE
• ¼ cup honey
• 1 tsp dried lavender or to taste

The heady scent of lavender in this tart evokes the hills of Provence in France. Use fresh lavender if you can find it or substitute rosemary or thyme for an equally intriguing flavor. For a pretty effect, do not peel the apples, but core and thinly slice them. The peel on the edge gives the cooked tart a colorful finish.

• Preheat the oven to 400°F. Using a swivel-bladed vegetable peeler, peel, core, and halve the apples. Place cut-side down on a work surface and cut crosswise into thin slices. Toss with 3–4 tablespoons of the wine and 2 tablespoons of the sugar.

• Starting at the outside edge, arrange the apple slices in overlapping concentric circles in the tart shell. Sprinkle with the remaining sugar. Bake until the apples are tender and the pastry crisp and golden, about 40 minutes. Transfer to a wire rack to cool slightly.

• In a small saucepan over medium-high heat, simmer the remaining wine, honey and lavender until reduced by half, about 5 minutes. Carefully brush the hot glaze over the tart. Serve warm.

SOUTHERN PECAN TART

• 9-inch tart pan lined with Basic Sweet Crust
(Pâte Sucrée) or Rich Pie Crust (Pâte Brisée Riche)

• 2½ cups pecan halves
• 3 eggs
• 1 cup packed dark brown sugar
• ¼ cup light corn syrup
• grated zest and juice of ½ lemon
• 4 tbsp butter, melted
• vanilla extract

This all-American classic pie looks even more stunning when baked in a tart pan. Serve warm with unsweetened whipped cream or sour cream or, of course, vanilla ice cream.

• Preheat the oven to 350°F. Pick out about 1 cup of perfect pecan halves and set aside. Coarsely chop the remaining nuts.

• Beat the eggs and sugar together until lightened. Beat in the corn syrup, grated lemon zest and juice, melted butter, vanilla extract, and the chopped pecans. Pour into the tart shell. Carefully set onto a baking sheet for easier handling.

• Arrange the perfect pecans in concentric circles on top of the egg-sugar mixture. Bake until the filling is set and slightly puffed and pecans are well colored, about 40 minutes. Transfer to a wire rack to cool slightly.

Right: Lavender-scented Apple Tart

PLUM CRUMBLE TARTS

. . . .

- Six 3½-inch tartlet pans, lined with Basic Sweet Crust (Pâte Sucrée), partially blind-baked

CRUMBLE TOPPING
- ¼ cup sugar
- ¼ cup light or dark brown sugar
- ⅔ cup all-purpose flour
- ¾ cup chopped walnuts or pecans
- ½ tsp ground cinnamon
- 5 tbsp cold butter, cut into small pieces

FILLING
- 1½ lbs plums
- 1 tbsp butter
- 2 tbsp sugar
- ½ tsp ground cinnamon
- lemon juice

. . . .

Almost any firm fruit can be substituted for the plums. The sharpness of the fruit contrasts perfectly with the sweet crumble topping.

- Prepare the crumble topping. Put the flour in a large bowl and sprinkle the pieces of butter over the top. Using a pastry blender, cut in the butter until the mixture resembles coarse crumbs. Do not overblend or the topping will be too dense. Stir in the sugars, nuts and cinnamon until well blended. Refrigerate until ready to use.

- Preheat the oven to 400°F. Halve the plums and, using a small spoon, remove the pits; chop coarsely. In a large skillet over medium-high heat, melt the butter. Add the plums and toss to coat. Sprinkle with the sugar and cinnamon, and cook for about 1 minute. Cool slightly.
- Divide the plum mixture equally among the tartlet shells and set them on a baking sheet for easier handling. Spoon the crumble mixture over the plums, mounding it generously. Bake 15–20 minutes until the topping is crisp and golden. Transfer tartlets to a wire rack to cool. Serve warm with crème fraîche, if liked.

BLUEBERRY CUSTARD TART

. . . .

- 10-inch tart pan lined with Basic Sweet Crust (Pâte Sucrée) or Extra Sweet Tart Crust (Pâte Sucrée Riche), partially blind-baked

- 1 lb fresh blueberries
- 1¼ cups whipping cream
- 3 eggs
- ¼ cup sugar
- ½ tsp almond or vanilla extract (optional)
- ¼ cup blueberry preserves or honey
- 1 tbsp water
- confectioners' sugar for dusting

. . . .

This delicious tart combines fresh and cooked blueberries for maximum flavor.

- Preheat the oven to 350°F. Set the tart shell on a baking sheet for easier handling. Reserve a quarter of the blueberries and set aside. Spread the remaining berries on the bottom of the tart shell.
- Beat the cream with the eggs and sugar until well blended. Stir in the almond or vanilla extract and carefully pour the custard mixture over the blueberries. Bake until a knife inserted 1 inch from the edges comes out clean, about 30 minutes.

Transfer to a wire rack to cool and set completely, about 30 minutes.
- In a small saucepan over medium heat, melt the preserves or honey with the water until smooth and bubbling. Drizzle over the remaining blueberries and toss to coat. Mound the berries onto the center of the tart and dust with confectioners' sugar. Serve warm or at room temperature.

Right: Plum Crumble Tarts

PEAR AND CHOCOLATE CREAM TART

......
- 9-inch tart pan lined with Extra Sweet Tart Crust (*Pâte Sucrée Riche*) or Chocolate Pastry

- 4 oz bittersweet chocolate, melted
- 1 cup whipping cream
- 4 tbsp sugar
- 1 egg
- 1 egg yolk
- 1 tsp vanilla or almond extract
- 3 medium ripe pears
......

Sweet ripe pears baked into a rich, chocolate, creamy custard are a heavenly combination.

- In a medium saucepan over low heat, melt the chocolate, cream and 2 tablespoons of the sugar, stirring frequently, until smooth. Remove from the heat and cool slightly. Beat in the egg, egg yolk, and vanilla extract and spread evenly in the tart shell. Set on a baking sheet for easier handling.
- Preheat the oven to 375°F. Using a swivel-bladed vegetable peeler, carefully peel, halve, and core the pears. Put them on a work surface cut-side down and cut crosswise into thin slices.

- Arrange the pears spoke fashion in the tart shell and press gently with the heel of your hand to fan out the pear slices towards the center. Tap the tart gently on the work surface to eliminate air bubbles.
- Bake for 10 minutes. Reduce the oven temperature to 350°F. Sprinkle the surface of the tart with the remaining sugar and bake until the custard is set and pears are tender and glazed, about 20 minutes more. Transfer to a wire rack to cool slightly. Serve warm.

CHERRY ALMOND TART

......
- 9-inch tart pan lined with Basic Sweet Crust (*Pâte Sucrée*)

- ½ cup dried tart cherries
- ½ cup water
- ⅔ cup blanched almonds
- 2 tbsp all-purpose flour
- 6 tbsp unsalted butter, softened
- sugar (see recipe)
- ½ tsp almond extract
- 1 egg
- 1 egg yolk
- 2 cups packed pitted fresh sweet cherries
- confectioners' sugar for dusting
......

In this tart, dried Michigan tart cherries, widely available in supermarkets, are combined with fresh cherries for maximum flavor.

- In a small saucepan, combine the dried cherries and water. Bring to a boil over medium-high heat. Reduce the heat and simmer over low heat until water is absorbed and cherries are soft and plump, about 15 minutes. Cool completely.
- Preheat the oven to 400°F. Put the almonds in a food processor fitted with a metal blade. Process until fine crumbs form. Add the flour and pulse to blend. Add the butter, ½ cup sugar, the almond extract, the egg, and egg yolk, and process

10–15 seconds until smooth and creamy, scraping down the sides of the bowl once. Spread the mixture evenly in the tart shell.
- In a bowl, combine the fresh cherries and plumped dried cherries and sprinkle with 2–3 tablespoons of sugar (or to taste). Toss well and spoon over the almond mixture, distributing the cherries evenly.
- Bake 15 minutes. Reduce the oven temperature to 350°F, sprinkle the surface with another teaspoon of sugar and continue baking until the filling is puffed and is golden, about 25 minutes longer. Transfer to a wire rack to cool slightly. Serve warm or at room temperature.

Right: Pear and Chocolate Cream Tart

TARTE TATIN

- ¾ lb store-bought puff pastry or 1 recipe
Basic Sweet Crust (Pâte Sucrée)

- 10 large Golden Delicious apples
- juice of 1 lemon
- 6 tbsp unsalted butter
- ¾ cup sugar
- ¼ tsp ground cinnamon
- crème fraîche or sour cream, for serving

This classic French tart was made famous by two sisters in a small town in France called Solonge; now it is served all over the world. It is equally delicious made with pears.

- On a lightly floured surface, roll out the pastry to an 11-inch circle, about ¼-inch thick. Slide onto a lightly floured baking sheet and refrigerate until needed.
- Using a swivel-bladed vegetable peeler, peel, core, and halve the apples. Sprinkle the apples with a little lemon juice as you work, to prevent them from darkening.
- In a 10-inch heavy-bottomed, ovenproof, deep skillet over medium-high heat, melt the butter. Add the sugar and cinnamon, stirring occasionally, until the sugar dissolves. Cook, stirring occasionally until the sugar is a rich golden caramel color. Remove from the heat.
- Carefully arrange the apple halves, rounded side down, around the outside edge of the pan, pressing them together tightly. Press the remaining apple halves into the center, squeezing them into a circle (remember the apples shrink as they cook). Be very careful not to touch the caramel as it is dangerously hot.

- Return the apple-filled pan to the heat and bring to a boil. Simmer until the apples begin to soften and the caramel darkens, about 20 minutes. Remove from the heat to cool slightly.
- Preheat the oven to 425°F. Remove the pastry round from the refrigerator and allow to soften slightly, about 5 minutes. Carefully slide the rolled-out dough circle over the apple-filled pan, centering the dough over the apples. Using a knife, carefully tuck the overhanging dough inside the edge of the pan. Pierce the dough in two or three places. Bake until golden, 25–30 minutes. Transfer to a wire rack to cool, about 5 minutes.
- Run a knife around the edge of the pan to release any pastry that might be stuck. Place a heatproof serving plate over the skillet and, using potholders, carefully invert them together (unmold this tart over the sink in case the caramel runs out). Gently remove the skillet, loosening any apple that may have stuck. Serve warm or at room temperature. Serve with crème fraîche or sour cream.

FIG AND CARAMELIZED-WALNUT TART

The flavor of figs and walnuts is emphasized further by the walnut crust. You can use a Basic Sweet Crust (Pâte Sucrée) if you prefer.

- Preheat the oven to 400°F. Quarter the figs and arrange them in concentric circles, cut-side up on the bottom of the tart. Bake until the figs just begin to soften, about 10 minutes. Transfer to a wire rack to cool slightly.

- In a medium skillet over medium-high heat, melt the butter and sugar. Cook, stirring occasionally, until a golden caramel color, 1–2 minutes. Add the walnuts and toss to coat, stirring constantly. Pour over the tart, tucking the walnuts between fig quarters.

- In a small saucepan over medium heat, heat the honey and lemon juice and brush or drizzle over the tart, cool slightly. Serve warm with the Greek yogurt or sour cream if liked.

SUMMER BERRY TART ON HAZELNUT CRUST

- 9-inch tart pan lined with Easy Nut Crust made with hazelnuts, blind-baked

- 1½ lbs mixed summer berries, such as strawberries, raspberries, loganberries, boysenberries, blueberries, red or black currants
- ⅓ cup red currant jelly or raspberry preserves
- 2 tbsp raspberry-flavor liqueur
- mint leaves for garnish (optional)

The nuttiness of the pastry goes beautifully with the sweetness of summer berries. If you like, substitute other favorite fruits cut into bite-sized pieces.

- Cut any large strawberries in half or quarters and put in a large bowl. Add the remaining fruit and toss just to combine.
- In a small saucepan over medium heat, heat the jelly or preserves with the liqueur until melted and smooth, stirring frequently. Drizzle over the fruit and shake the bowl to help lightly coat the fruit.

- Pour the fruit mixture into the tart shell, gently distributing fruit evenly over surface and into edge. If you like, garnish with fresh mint leaves.

DRIED APRICOT AND AMARETTO CREAM TART

- 9-inch tart pan lined with Extra Sweet Tart Crust (*Pâte Sucrée Riche*), partially blind-baked

- ⅔ cup blanched almonds
- ⅓ cup sugar, or to taste
- ½ lb cream cheese, softened
- 6 tbsp butter, softened
- 2 eggs
- 4–5 tbsp Amaretto liqueur
- ½ lb ready-to-eat dried apricots, halved
- 2 tbsp apricot preserves

The flavor of dried apricots is more intense than fresh and they are always available. For a change, use a cookie crumb crust made with half Graham crackers and half crushed Amaretto cookies.

- Preheat the oven to 375°F. In a food processor fitted with the metal blade, process the almonds with half the sugar until very fine crumbs form. Add the remaining sugar, cream cheese, butter, eggs, and 2 tablespoons of the Amaretto, and process until smooth and creamy, 20–30 seconds. Spread evenly on the bottom of the tart shell. Set on a baking sheet for easier handling.

- Arrange the apricot halves over the filling, pressing them into the mixture, but not completely submerging them. Bake until the filling is set and golden, about 25 minutes. Transfer to a wire rack to cool slightly.
- In a small saucepan over medium heat, heat the preserves with the remaining liqueur until smooth and melted. Brush over the top of the tart. Serve warm.

Right: Summer Berry Tart on Hazelnut Crust

STRAWBERRY HEART TART

. . . .
- 10 oz store-bought puff pastry

- 1½ lbs strawberries
- ½ cup red currant jelly
- 2 tbsp Kirsch, cherry-flavor liqueur, or water (optional)

. . . .

A heart-shaped cake pan can be used to make this tart, carefully unmolding the pastry before filling. Alternatively, a free-form heart shape can be made on a baking sheet.

● Lightly spray a 9-inch heart-shaped cake pan with vegetable oil. On a lightly floured surface, roll out the dough to a circle about ⅛-inch thick. Line the cake pan with the pastry, pressing into the base. Trim and crimp the edges.
● Preheat the oven to 425°F. Line the heart-shaped dough with foil and fill with beans. Blind bake 10–15 minutes. Reduce the oven temperature to 400°F, remove foil and beans and continue baking until crisp and golden brown, about 15 minutes longer. Transfer to a wire rack to cool completely. Carefully remove the pastry heart from the pan.
● Cut off the stem end of the strawberries and slice each lengthwise. If they have a rounded not pointed tip, cut them through the narrowest part to make them appear more pointed. Arrange them, tightly together, pointed ends up, in the tart shell.
● In a small saucepan over medium heat, heat the jelly with the liqueur or 2 tablespoons water until melted and bubbling. Cool slightly, then brush the berries with a thick layer of glaze, allowing it to dribble between the berries. Serve at room temperature.

SIMPLE ALMOND TART

. . . .
- 10-inch square tart pan lined with Almond-Enriched Basic Sweet Crust *(Pâte Sucrée)*, blind-baked and still warm

- 6 tbsp unsalted butter, softened
- ½ cup sugar
- 3 tbsp whipping cream
- 1¼ cups flaked or slivered blanched almonds, lightly toasted
- whipped cream or vanilla ice cream for serving

. . . .

This tart is based on those made in Spain and Portugal, where white-blossomed almond trees cover the hills in the spring.

● Preheat the oven to 425°F and line a large baking sheet with foil. With an electric mixer on high speed, beat the butter, sugar, and cream until light and fluffy, about 5 minutes. Gently fold in 1 cup of the almonds and spread evenly over the bottom of the warm tart shell; sprinkle with the remaining almonds. Set the tart on the baking sheet for easier handling.
● Bake the tart until the filling is bubbling and caramelized, and tart is golden, 15–18 minutes. Transfer to a wire rack to cool completely (be careful since the caramelized filling is very hot). Serve at room temperature with whipped cream or ice cream.

Right: Strawberry Heart Tart

MANGO GALETTES

. . . .
- 1 recipe Extra Sweet Tart Crust
  (Pâte Sucrée Riche)

- 2 medium ripe mangoes
- 1 tbsp unsalted butter, melted
- 2 tbsp superfine sugar
- 2 tbsp apricot preserves or honey
. . . .

This idea can be used with any tender fruit which cooks quickly, such as nectarines, peaches, or even papayas (paw-paw). Puff pastry also makes an easy base.

- On a lightly floured surface, roll out the pastry ¼ inch thick. Using a large fluted cutter or saucer as a guide, cut out six 4-inch circles, re-rolling pastry scraps if necessary. Transfer to a large baking sheet, scallop the edges if you like and prick the bases to within ⅜ inch of the edge. Refrigerate 30 minutes.

- Preheat the oven to 400°F. Peel the mangoes. Cut off each half and lay cut sides down. Slice crosswise, thinly.
- Arrange the mango slices over the pastry circles to within ⅜ inch of the edge. Brush with a little melted butter and sprinkle each with a quarter of the sugar. Bake until the mango begins to caramelize and pastry is set and golden, about 15 minutes. Transfer to a wire rack to cool slightly.
- In a small saucepan over medium heat, melt the apricot preserves or honey. Brush over the galettes and serve warm.

RASPBERRY 'N' CREAM TARTS

. . . .
- Six 3-inch tartlet pans lined with Extra Sweet Tart Crust *(Pâte Sucrée Riche)*, blind-baked

- 1 cup milk
- ½ vanilla bean or 1 tsp vanilla extract
- 3 egg yolks
- ¼ cup sugar
- 1 tbsp all-purpose flour
- 1 tbsp cornstarch
- 1 tbsp butter, diced
- ⅓ cup whipping cream (optional)
- 1½ lbs raspberries
- ¼ cup seedless raspberry preserves
- 1 tbsp framboise or raspberry-flavored liqueur
. . . .

This delicious pastry cream can be used as a base for any fruit tart. Do not assemble too far ahead as the pastry will soften.

- Pour all but 2 tablespoons milk into a medium saucepan. Split the vanilla bean and scrape the seeds into the milk with the bean. Bring to a boil over medium heat and set aside to infuse 15 minutes.
- Beat the egg yolks with the sugar until thick and light in color, 3–4 minutes. Gently stir in the flour, cornstarch, and the reserved 2 tablespoons milk to form a thick smooth paste.
- Remove the vanilla bean and bring the milk back to a boil. Slowly whisk into the egg mixture until well blended, then return the milk and egg mixture to the pan and cook, stirring constantly, over

medium-low heat to thicken. Once thickened, increase the heat to medium-high and allow the custard to boil, about 2 minutes, stirring constantly. Scrape into a bowl and, if using vanilla extract, stir in at this point. Immediately sprinkle with the diced butter. Cool completely.
- If using the cream, beat until soft peaks form. Beat the cooled pastry cream to loosen it, then fold in the whipped cream. Spread a thick layer on the bottom of each tartlet shell and cover with raspberries.
- In a small saucepan over medium heat, heat the preserves and liqueur until melted and bubbling. Brush or spoon lightly over the raspberries. These tartlets are best served at room temperature.

Right: Mango Galettes

SUMMER FRUIT PIZZA TART

- 1 recipe Basic Sweet Crust (*Pâte Sucrée*) or Walnut- or Almond-Enriched Basic Sweet Crust

- 2 tbsp honey
- 1 small peach, thinly sliced
- 1 small nectarine, thinly sliced
- 1 cup strawberries, halved or quartered
- ½ cup raspberries
- ½ cup blackberries
- ½ cup blueberries
- 1 tbsp melted butter
- 2–3 tbsp sugar

This freeform tart resembles a pizza — cover it with any soft fruit you like. It's delicious with ice cream!

● Lightly spray or brush a large baking sheet with vegetable oil. On a lightly floured surface, roll out the dough to an 11- or 12-inch circle, about ⅛ inch thick. Transfer to the baking sheet. Crimp the edge and prick the bottom all over. Refrigerate 30 minutes.

● Preheat the oven to 400°F. Line the dough circle with foil and weight with the bottom of a tart pan or ovenproof dinner plate. Bake 10 minutes until the pastry edge begins to color. Remove the weight and foil.

● Gently brush the surface with the honey and arrange the fruits in triangles or circles over the surface of the pastry. Brush the fruit with the melted butter and sprinkle with the sugar.

● Bake until the fruit is tender and pastry is golden, about 5–7 minutes. If you like, turn on the broiler and broil the tart until the fruit begins to caramelize, 1–2 minutes. Cover the edge of the pastry with foil if it browns too quickly. Cool slightly and serve warm.

MINI-PINE NUT TARTLETS IN CREAM CHEESE PASTRY

- 1 recipe Cream Cheese Pastry

- 1 egg
- ½ cup packed light to dark brown sugar
- 1 tbsp light corn syrup
- 1½ tbsp unsalted butter, melted
- 1 cup pine nuts, lightly toasted

Cream Cheese Pastry has a lovely rich flavor and tender texture which goes beautifully with this sugary pine nut filling. Try pecans, walnuts or macadamias as well.

● Lightly spray or brush with vegetable oil 2 x 12-cup or 1 x 24-cup muffin pans. On a lightly floured surface, roll out the dough ⅛-inch thick. Using a 2½-inch fluted cutter, cut out 24 circles. Carefully line the muffin-pan cups, pressing the dough into the edge of each cup. Refrigerate 30 minutes.

● Preheat the oven to 350°F. Beat the egg until foamy. Gradually beat in the brown sugar, corn syrup, and melted butter. Stir in three-quarters of the pine nuts and carefully fill each muffin cup with the mixture. Sprinkle with pine nuts.

● Bake the tartlets until the filling is set and pastry edges are golden, about 20 minutes. Transfer the muffin pans or pan to a wire rack to cool at least 20 minutes. Using the tip of a knife, loosen the pastry from each cup and unmold each tartlet. Serve at room temperature.

Right: Summer Fruit Pizza Tart

MACADAMIA TARTLETS

. . . .

- Twelve 3½-inch tartlet pans lined with Basic Sweet Crust (*Pâte Sucrée*), partially blind-baked

- 2 eggs
- ¼ cup sugar
- ¾ cup light corn syrup
- 3 tbsp butter, melted
- 3 tbsp whipping cream
- 1 tbsp orange-flavored liqueur
- ¼ cup candied orange peel chopped
- 2 cups unsalted macadamia nuts, coarsely chopped
- 4 oz semisweet or bittersweet chocolate, melted (optional)

. . . .

These tartlets make a delicious dessert served with vanilla ice cream. Make them in tiny mini-tartlet molds to serve with after-dinner coffee.

- Preheat the oven to 350°F. Arrange the tartlets on a large baking sheet for easier handling.
- Whisk the eggs and sugar together until light and foamy, about 1 minute. Whisk in the corn syrup, butter, cream, and liqueur, then stir in the orange peel and nuts.

- Divide the mixture evenly among the tartlets. Bake until the filling is set, about 20 minutes. Transfer to a wire rack to cool completely. If you like, drizzle or pipe each tartlet with a little melted chocolate. Serve at room temperature.

NECTARINE SHORTBREAD TART

. . . .

SHORTBREAD PASTRY
- 1½ cups all-purpose flour
- ⅓ cup sugar
- ½ tsp ground cinnamon
- ½ cup (1 stick) butter, at room temperature, cut into small pieces

FILLING
- 1½ lbs nectarines, pitted and sliced
- ½ tsp almond extract
- 2–3 tbsp sugar
- 2 tbsp flour
- ½ tsp ground cinnamon
- ¼ cup slivered almonds

. . . .

This tart uses a quick, shortbread-type pastry that does not need chilling or rolling. It is equally delicious with plums or peaches.

- Preheat the oven to 375°F. Lightly spray or oil a 9-inch tart pan with a vegetable spray or oil.
- In a large bowl, stir together the flour, sugar, and cinnamon. Sprinkle over the pieces of butter and, using a pastry blender, cut in the butter until a soft dough begins to form. Turn into the tart pan and, using your fingertips, press the dough evenly onto the bottom and up the side of the pan.

- In a bowl, toss the nectarine slices with the almond extract, sugar (to taste), flour, and cinnamon. Starting at the outside edge, arrange the slices in overlapping concentric circles in the tart shell. Sprinkle with the almonds.
- Set the tart shell on a baking sheet for easier handling. Bake until the nectarines are tender and pastry is golden and crisp, about 35–40 minutes. Rotate the tart halfway through cooking time if it begins to color unevenly. Transfer to a wire rack to cool slightly. Serve warm, at room temperature, or cold.

Right: Macadamia Tartlets

chapter five

CHOCOLATE, CUSTARD, AND CREAM TARTS

LEMON TART

This is one of my favorite tarts, a creamy sweet-sharp lemon filling encased in crisp tender pastry — simple but delicious.

● Preheat the oven to 375°F. With an electric mixer on low speed, beat together the lemon zest, juice, and sugar. Slowly beat in the cream or crème fraîche until blended, then beat in the eggs and yolks, one at a time.

● Set the tart shell on a baking sheet for easier handling and carefully pour in the filling. (If you prefer a completely smooth filling, strain into the tart shell, removing the zest.)

● Bake until the filling is just set, but not colored, about 20 minutes. If the tart begins to color, cover with foil. Transfer to a wire rack to cool completely. Dust with confectioners' sugar before serving.

. . . .
- 9- or 10-inch tart pan lined with Extra Sweet Tart Crust *(Pâte Brisée Riche)*, partially blind-baked

- grated zest of 2–3 lemons
- ⅔ cup freshly squeezed lemon juice
- ½ cup sugar
- ½ cup whipping cream or crème fraîche
- 3 eggs
- 3 egg yolks
- confectioners' sugar, for dusting
. . . .

LIME CURD PHYLLO TARTLETS WITH RASPBERRIES

- 4 sheets phyllo dough, defrosted if frozen

- 2 tbsp unsalted butter, melted
- sugar
- 2 eggs, beaten
- ½ cup (1 stick) unsalted butter, diced
- ½ cup sugar
- 2 tbsp freshly grated lime zest
- ¼ cup freshly squeezed lime juice (about 1–2 limes)
- 1 lb fresh raspberries
- fresh mint sprigs for garnish (optional)

A delicious tangy lime curd makes an ideal filling for these crisp phyllo cups. The raspberries add a stunning color as well as flavor contrast.

● Preheat the oven to 350°F. Lightly oil four ¾-cup ramekins with vegetable oil. Cut the phyllo dough sheets into 6-inch squares. Keep the phyllo dough covered with a damp dishtowel to prevent the dough from drying out.

● Place a phyllo square on the work surface, brush with a little melted butter, and sprinkle with a little sugar. Butter a second square and lay it over the first square at an angle; sprinkle with a little sugar. Repeat with two more phyllo squares. Press the stack of squares into a custard cup or ramekin, pressing into the edge and keeping the edges turned up. Continue to line the remaining ramekins.

● Set the cups on a baking sheet for easier handling. Bake until crisp and golden, about 10 minutes. Transfer to a wire rack and cool completely.

● In a medium saucepan, combine the eggs, butter, ½ cup sugar, lime zest, and juice. Cook over medium-low heat until the mixture begins to thicken and bubbles begin to appear on the surface, about 3 minutes. Scrape into a bowl and cover with plastic wrap, pressing the wrap against the surface of the curd to prevent a skin from forming. Refrigerate at least 1 hour.

● Put half the raspberries and 2–3 tablespoons of sugar in a food processor fitted with the metal blade and process until smooth. Strain into a bowl and stir in the remaining berries. Divide the curd mixture evenly among the phyllo cups. Top each with some of the raspberry sauce; serve the remaining sauce separately. Garnish with mint.

DOUBLE CHOCOLATE TRUFFLE TARTS

- Eight 4-inch tartlet pans lined with Chocolate Pastry, blind-baked

- 1¼ cups whipping cream
- 10 oz bittersweet chocolate, chopped
- 2 tbsp unsalted butter
- ¼ cup Cognac, brandy, or other favorite liqueur
- unsweetened cocoa powder for dusting

Rich and sophisticated, this makes an elegant dessert presentation.

● In a medium saucepan over medium-high heat, bring the cream to a boil. Remove from the heat and add the chocolate, stirring until completely melted. Beat in the butter and stir in the Cognac or brandy. Strain the mixture into a measuring cup or pitcher.

● Divide the mixture evenly among the tartlet shells, smoothing the tops so they are completely flat. Refrigerate 3–4 hours or overnight.

● Cut out strips of waxed paper about ⅜ inch wide. Place in a random pattern over a tartlet and dust with cocoa. Repeat with the remaining tartlets. Remove from the refrigerator about 15 minutes before serving.

Right: Lime Curd Phyllo Tartlets with Raspberries

PUMPKIN TART WITH PECAN PRALINE TOPPING

- 9-inch tart pan lined with Basic Sweet Crust (*Pâte Sucrée*), partially blind-baked

- 1¼ cups canned solid-packed pumpkin
  - ½ cup sugar
  - ¼ cup packed light brown sugar
  - ¾ cup whipping cream
  - ⅓ cup milk
  - 2 eggs
- 1–2 tbsp bourbon or whisky (optional)
  - ¾ tsp ground cinnamon
  - ½ tsp allspice
  - ½ tsp ground ginger
  - ¼ tsp ground cloves
  - ¼ tsp grated nutmeg

TOPPING
- ½ cup chopped pecans
- ½ cup packed light brown sugar
- 2 tbsp unsalted butter, melted
- whipped cream or vanilla ice cream for serving

This is the traditional Thanksgiving pumpkin pie with a face lift. The pecan topping is easy to make and adds a crunchy contrast to the creamy filling.

● Preheat the oven to 350°F. With an electric mixer, beat the pumpkin with the remaining ingredients (except the topping and whipped cream) until smooth and well-blended. Set the tart on a baking sheet for easier handling and carefully pour the mixture into the tart shell.

● Bake until the filling is just set (tart will continue to cook once removed) and pastry is golden, about 45 minutes. Cover the pastry edge with foil if it browns too quickly. Remove to a wire rack to cool completely; then refrigerate.
● Preheat the broiler. Combine the pecans, sugar, and butter, and sprinkle evenly over the tart. Cover the edge of the pastry with a strip of foil if necessary. Broil about 4 inches from the heat until the topping bubbles and caramelizes, watching carefully, about 1 minute. Allow to cool, then serve the tart at room temperature or cold with whipped cream or ice cream if desired.

GINGERED CRÈME BRULÉE TARTLETS

These delicately flavored tartlets will soon become one of your favorites. The thick custard can be flavored by infusing the cream with a split vanilla bean if you prefer, but the ginger adds a subtle Eastern flavor.

● Preheat the oven to 325°F. Set the tartlet shells on a baking sheet for easier handling.

● In a small saucepan over medium heat, bring the cream to a boil. Whisk the egg and egg yolks with the sugar and ginger syrup until lightened, about 1 minute. Slowly whisk in the hot cream, stirring constantly. Strain into a measuring jug or pitcher and stir in the chopped ginger.

● Divide the mixture evenly among the tartlet shells. Bake until the custard is lightly set, about 15 minutes. Transfer to a wire rack to cool, then refrigerate at least 4 hours or overnight.

● Just before serving, preheat the broiler. Sprinkle a thin layer of sugar evenly over the custard right to the pastry edge. If the pastry is already very brown, protect with a thin strip of foil while broiling. Broil close to the heat until the sugar melts and begins to bubble, about 1 minute. Do not over-broil or the custard will begin to curdle. Refrigerate immediately to allow the caramel to harden, about 5 minutes; then serve.

. . . .

● Four 4-inch tartlet pans lined with Basic Sweet Crust *(Pâte Sucrée)* or Ginger Crumb Crust, blind-baked

● 1¼ cups whipping cream
● 1 egg
● 2 egg yolks
● 1 tbsp sugar
● 1 tbsp ginger syrup (from the bottle)
● 1 piece bottled stem ginger, finely chopped
● 4–6 tbsp golden granulated sugar

. . . .

CHOCOLATE GANACHE AND BERRY TART

. . . .

- 9-inch tart pan lined with Chocolate Pastry, blind-baked

- 2¾ cups whipping cream
- 1 cup seedless raspberry preserves
- ½ lb good quality bittersweet chocolate, chopped
- ¼ cup framboise or raspberry-flavored liqueur
- 1½ lbs mixed fresh summer berries, such as raspberries, blackberries, strawberries (quartered if large), loganberries, or blueberries
- 1–2 tbsp superfine sugar

. . . .

Summer berries make a perfect match for a rich chocolate tart shell filled with a dark chocolate and raspberry truffle mixture.

● In a medium saucepan over medium heat, bring 1¼ cups of the cream and three-quarters of the raspberry preserves to a boil, whisking to dissolve the preserves. Remove from the heat and add the chocolate all at once, stirring until melted and smooth. Strain the mixture directly into the tart shell, lifting and turning the tart to distribute the filling evenly. Cool completely or refrigerate until set, at least 1 hour.

● In a small saucepan over medium heat, heat the remaining raspberry preserves and 2 tablespoons of the framboise or raspberry-flavor liqueur until melted and bubbling. Drizzle over the berries and toss to coat well. Arrange the berries over the top of the tart. Refrigerate until ready to serve.

● Bring the tart to room temperature at least ½ hour before serving. Whip the remaining cream with the sugar and remaining framboise- or raspberry-flavored liqueur until soft peaks form. Spoon into a serving bowl and serve with the tart.

IRISH CREAM BARQUETTES

. . . .

- 12 mini barquettes or other mini-tartlet pans lined with Extra Sweet Tart Crust (*Pâte Sucrée Riche*), blind-baked

- 4 oz semisweet chocolate, melted
- ½ cup milk
- 3 egg yolks
- 2 tbsp sugar
- 3 tbsp all-purpose flour
- ¼ cup Irish Cream liqueur
- ¼ cup whipping cream, whipped
- chocolate shavings or unsweetened cocoa powder, for dusting

. . . .

These little tartlets make an ideal accompaniment to an after-dinner coffee. Use other shapes to form the tartlets, such as hearts, squares, or circles.

● Brush the bottom of each tartlet with a little melted chocolate. Set the tartlets on a baking sheet for easier handling.

● In a heavy-bottomed saucepan over medium heat, bring the milk just to a boil. Beat the egg yolks and sugar until light, about 1 minute and stir in the flour. Add the hot milk whisking constantly.

● Return the custard to the heat and cook, until it thickens, about 2 minutes, whisking constantly. Remove from the heat and whisk in the Irish cream liqueur. Allow to cool. Gently fold in the cream and refrigerate until thickened, about 30 minutes.

● Spoon the custard-cream into a decorating bag fitted with a medium star tip. Pipe into the tartlet shells and refrigerate. Garnish with chocolate shavings or dust with cocoa just before serving.

Right: Chocolate Ganache and Berry Tart

CHOCOLATE SOUFFLÉ TARTS

- 6–8 brioche molds or other deep tartlet pans or ramekins, buttered and lined with Chocolate Pastry or Rich Pie Crust (*Pâte Brisée Riche*), blind-baked

- 4 oz bittersweet or semisweet chocolate, chopped
- ¼ cup (½ stick) butter
- 4 eggs, separated
- 2 tbsp brandy or Cognac
- ¼ tsp cream of tartar
- 2 tbsp sugar
- confectioners' sugar for dusting

These baked cases can be used to hold a mousse or other creamy tart fillings. If using chocolate pastry or other butter-rich pastry, leave the cases in the molds as they will melt down when rebaked with the soufflé mixture.

● Preheat the oven to 425°F. Set the tartlet molds or ramekins on a baking sheet for easier handling.

● In a saucepan over low heat, melt the chocolate and butter until smooth, stirring frequently. Remove from the heat and beat in the egg yolks, one at a time, then beat in the brandy. Set aside.

● In a large bowl with an electric mixer, beat the egg whites and cream of tartar until soft peaks form. Sprinkle in the sugar, a tablespoon at a time, and continue beating until stiff peaks form.

● Stir a spoonful of whites into the chocolate mixture to lighten it, then fold in the remaining whites. Divide the mixture evenly among the tartlets, filling them almost to the pastry edge. Bake 10–12 minutes until the mixture is just set, but still slightly wobbly. Dust with confectioners' sugar and serve immediately.

MOCHA MOUSSE SLICE

- 14 x 4-inch tart pan lined with Extra Sweet Tart Crust (*Pâte Sucrée Riche*) or Chocolate Pastry, blind-baked

- 8 oz bittersweet chocolate, chopped
- ¼ cup strong coffee
- ¼ cup (½ stick) butter
- 2 tbsp coffee-flavored liqueur or rum
- 3 eggs, separated
- ¼ tsp cream of tartar
- 1 oz white chocolate, melted, for decoration (optional)

WARNING: contains uncooked egg whites.

A delicious way to serve a luscious chocolate mousse. For a special effect, decorate with white chocolate.

● In a medium saucepan over medium-low heat, melt the chocolate and coffee until smooth, stirring frequently. Remove from the heat and beat in the butter and liqueur. Beat in the egg yolks, one at a time, until the mixture thickens.

● In a large bowl with an electric mixer, beat the egg whites and cream of tartar until soft peaks form. Beat a large spoonful of whites into the chocolate mixture to lighten it, then fold in the remaining whites. Pour into the tart shell.

● Make a paper cone: fold a square of waxed paper in half to form a triangle. With the middle triangle point facing you, fold the left corner down to the center. Fold the right corner down and wrap completely round the left corner, forming a cone.

● Spoon the melted white chocolate into the cone and fold the top edge over to enclose it. Snip off the point of the cone to make a hole about ⅛ inch across. Pipe parallel lines of white chocolate crosswise across the chocolate mousse surface. Using a wooden skewer draw across the white chocolate to feather the lines. Refrigerate 2–3 hours or overnight to set completely.

Right: Chocolate Soufflé Tarts

ORANGE CARDAMOM TART

- 9-inch tart pan lined with Extra Sweet Tart Crust (*Pâte Sucrée Riche*), partially blind-baked

- 5 tbsp fine-cut orange marmalade
- sugar
- 1¼ cups freshly squeezed orange juice, strained
- 2 large navel oranges, thinly sliced
- ½ cup (1 stick) unsalted butter, softened
- 2 eggs
- 2 egg yolks
- ⅔ cup whipping cream
- seeds from 4–5 cardamom pods, lightly crushed
- grated zest of 3 oranges
- ¼ cup golden raisins, plumped

This delicious orange tart is flavored with cardamom seeds, which give it a slightly exotic touch. Topped with orange slices, it looks stunning.

- In a small saucepan over low heat, heat 3 tablespoons of the marmalade until melted. Use to brush the bottom of the tart shell with an even layer. Set on a baking sheet for easier handling.
- In a medium saucepan, combine ¾ cup sugar and 1 cup of the orange juice. Bring to a boil and cook until thick and syrupy, about 10 minutes. Add the orange slices to the syrup and simmer gently until completely glazed, about 10 minutes. Carefully transfer to a rack set over a baking sheet to catch any drips. Reserve the syrup.

- Preheat the oven to 375°F. With an electric mixer, beat the butter, eggs, and egg yolks, and ¾ cup sugar until lightened, about 2 minutes. Gradually beat in the cream, cardamom seeds, and remaining marmalade. Stir in the orange zest, remaining juice, and the raisins. (Mixture may look curdled but it will be fine.)
- Pour the mixture into the tart shell. Bake until the filling is just set, about 35 minutes. Transfer to a wire rack to cool slightly. Arrange the orange slices in overlapping concentric circles on top of the tart. Bring the reserved syrup to a boil and brush over the orange slices to glaze. Serve at room temperature.

FLORIDA KEY LIME TART

- 9-inch tart pan or pie plate lined with Ginger Crumb Crust

- 3 large egg yolks
- 1 x 14-oz can sweetened condensed milk
- ½ cup Key lime or freshly squeezed lime juice (about 3 limes)
- 1 tbsp grated lime zest
- 1 cup whipping cream

Originally made with the small, yellowish limes from the Florida Keys, this tart can be made with any limes. Florida key lime juice is available in bottles from larger supermarkets and some specialty stores.

- With an electric mixer, beat the egg yolks until thick and creamy, about 3 minutes. Gradually beat in the condensed milk, lime juice, and zest. Pour into the tart shell and refrigerate until completely set, at least 4 hours or overnight.

- Beat the cream until stiff peaks form. Spoon the cream into a decorating bag fitted with a medium star tip and pipe a decorative border between the outer edge and center. Alternatively, serve cold with whipped cream passed separately. WARNING: People with weak immune systems, or pregnant women may wish to avoid this dish because it contains uncooked egg.

INDEX